Nantawan B. Lewis
Marie M. Fortune
Editors

Remembering Conquest: Feminist/Womanist Perspectives on Religion, Colonization, and Sexual Violence

Remembering Conquest: Feminist/Womanist Perspectives on Religion, Colonization, and Sexual Violence has been co-published simultaneously as *Journal of Religion & Abuse*, Volume 1, Number 2 1999.

*Pre-Publication
REVIEWS,
COMMENTARIES,
EVALUATIONS . . .*

"**A** book of extraordinary courage. The stories told are deeply moving and disturbing. The authors break new ground in probing different shades of meaning of colonialism and how it intersects with sexual violence, global racism, and late capitalism. The cross-cultural discussion provides astute analyses of the ambiguous roles religion plays in supporting white supremacy and male control. A must read for anyone interested in moving beyond the dominance of white feminist discourse on sexuality and committed to social transformation of women's lives in a global context."

Kwok Pui-lan, ThD
*William F. Cole Professor
of Christian Theology and Spirituality
Episcopal Divinity School*

"**T**his book is disturbing, important, and illuminating. Its essays explore sexual violence as a weapon of American neocolonialism and white supremacy.

Women from Thailand, the Philippines, African American and Native American communities analyze the destructive impact of colonialism that targets the bodies and minds of women as a means to control whole peoples. The authors explore the deep roots of misogyny in native and imported religious traditions, but they also find in those traditions resources for imagining a different reality.

The book is both chilling and hopeful as only prophetic truth-telling can be. It hurts the eyes and the soul. Implicitly it cries for profound culture conversion in the United States and among religious peoples."

Kathleen M. O'Connor, PhD
Professor of Old Testament
Columbia Theological Seminary

Remembering Conquest: Feminist/Womanist Perspectives on Religion, Colonization, and Sexual Violence

Remembering Conquest: Feminist/Womanist Perspectives on Religion, Colonization, and Sexual Violence has been co-published simultaneously as *Journal of Religion & Abuse,* Volume 1, Number 2 1999.

The *Journal of Religion & Abuse* Monographic "Separates"

Below is a list of "separates," which in serials librarianship means a special issue simultaneously published as a special journal issue or double-issue *and* as a "separate" hardbound monograph. (This is a format which we also call a "DocuSerial.")

"Separates" are published because specialized libraries or professionals may wish to purchase a specific thematic issue by itself in a format which can be separately cataloged and shelved, as opposed to purchasing the journal on an on-going basis. Faculty members may also more easily consider a "separate" for classroom adoption.

"Separates" are carefully classified separately with the major book jobbers so that the journal tie-in can be noted on new book order slips to avoid duplicate purchasing.

You may wish to visit Haworth's Website at . . .

http://www.haworthpressinc.com

. . . to search our online catalog for complete tables of contents of these separates and related publications.

You may also call 1-800-HAWORTH (outside US/Canada: 607-722-5857), or Fax 1-800-895-0582 (outside US/Canada: 607-771-0012), or e-mail at:

getinfo@haworthpressinc.com

Remembering Conquest: Feminist/Womanist Perspectives on Religion, Colonization, and Sexual Violence, edited by Nantawan Boonprasat Lewis, BDiv, ThM, PhD, and Marie M. Fortune, MDiv, DHLit (Vol. 1, No. 2, 1999). *Addresses the issue of sexual violence against Native American, African American, Filipino, and Thai women from feminist/womanist theological perspectives and advocates for change in how some religious groups interpret women.*

Remembering Conquest: Feminist/Womanist Perspectives on Religion, Colonization, and Sexual Violence

Nantawan Boonprasat Lewis, BDiv, ThM, PhD
Marie M. Fortune, MDiv, DHLit
Editors

Remembering Conquest: Feminist/Womanist Perspectives on Religion, Colonization, and Sexual Violence has been co-published simultaneously as *Journal of Religion & Abuse,* Volume 1, Number 2 1999.

The Haworth Pastoral Press
An Imprint of
The Haworth Press, Inc.
New York • London • Oxford

Published by

The Haworth Pastoral Press, 10 Alice Street, Binghamton, NY 13904-1580, USA

The Haworth Pastoral Press is an imprint of The Haworth Press, Inc., 10 Alice Street, Binghamton, NY 13904-1580 USA.

Remembering Conquest: Feminist/Womanist Perspectives on Religion, Colonization, and Sexual Violence has been co-published simultaneously as *Journal of Religion & Abuse,* Volume 1, Number 2 1999.

Cover design by Thomas J. Mayshock Jr.

Library of Congress Cataloging-in-Publication Data

Remembering conquest: feminist/womanist perspectives on religion, colonization, and sexual violence / Nantawan Boonprasat Lewis, Marie M. Fortune, editors.
  p. cm.
  Includes bibliographical references and index.
  ISBN 0-7890-0796-7 (alk. paper) – ISBN 0-7890-0829-7 (alk. paper)
  1. Minority women–United States–Social conditions. 2. Women–Developing countries–Social conditions. 3. Sex crimes–United States–History. 4. Missions, American–History. 5. United States–Territorial expansion. 6. Imperialism. I. Boonprasat Lewis, Nantawan. II. Fortune, Marie M.

HQ1410.R46 1999
305.42′09172′4--dc21

                   99-046046

INDEXING & ABSTRACTING

Contributions to this publication are selectively indexed or abstracted in print, electronic, online, or CD-ROM version(s) of the reference tools and information services listed below. This list is current as of the copyright date of this publication. See the end of this section for additional notes.

- *Abstracts of Research in Pastoral Care & Counseling*

- *CNPIEC Reference Guide: Chinese National Directory of Foreign Periodicals*

- *Contemporary Women's Issues*

- *Criminal Justice Abstracts*

- *Family Studies Database*

- *Family Violence & Sexual Assault Bulletin*

- *Guide to Social Science & Religion*

- *IBZ International Bibliography of Periodical Literature*

- *Index to Periodical Articles Related to Law*

- *National Clearinghouse on Child Abuse & Neglect*

- *Orere Source, The (Pastoral Abstracts)*

- *Peace Research Abstracts Journal*

- *Referativnyi Zhurnal (Abstracts Journal of the All-Russian Institute of Scientific and Technical Information)*

- *Theology Digest*

- *Women's Resources International Abstracts*

(continued)

*Special Bibliographic Notes related to special journal issues
(separates) and indexing/abstracting:*

- indexing/abstracting services in this list will also cover material in any "separate" that is co-published simultaneously with Haworth's special thematic journal issue or DocuSerial. Indexing/abstracting usually covers material at the article/chapter level.
- monographic co-editions are intended for either non-subscribers or libraries which intend to purchase a second copy for their circulating collections.
- monographic co-editions are reported to all jobbers/wholesalers/approval plans. The source journal is listed as the "series" to assist the prevention of duplicate purchasing in the same manner utilized for books-in-series.
- to facilitate user/access services all indexing/abstracting services are encouraged to utilize the co-indexing entry note indicated at the bottom of the first page of each article/chapter/contribution.
- this is intended to assist a library user of any reference tool (whether print, electronic, online, or CD-ROM) to locate the monographic version if the library has purchased this version but not a subscription to the source journal.
- individual articles/chapters in any Haworth publication are also available through the Haworth Document Delivery Service (HDDS).

Remembering Conquest: Feminist/Womanist Perspectives on Religion, Colonization, and Sexual Violence

CONTENTS

ABOUT THE EDITORS

Nantawan Boonprasat Lewis, BDiv, ThM, PhD, teaches religious studies and ethnic studies at Metropolitan State University in St. Paul/ Minneapolis, Minnesota. Her forthcoming book is *Poverty, Sexual Slavery and AIDS: Reconstructing Asian Feminist Theology of Liberation* from William B. Eerdmans Publishing.

Marie M. Fortune, MDiv, DHLit, is Founder and Executive Director of the Center for the Prevention of Sexual and Domestic Violence in Seattle, Washington, an educational ministry serving as a training resource to religious communities in the United States and Canada. A pastor, educator, and practicing ethicist and theologian, she is the author of several books, including *Is Nothing Sacred? When Sex Invades the Pastoral Relationship*, which won the 1990 Book of the Year Award from the Academy of Parish Clergy. Rev. Fortune received her seminary training at Yale Divinity School and was ordained a minister in the United Church of Christ in 1976. She has been recognized for her dedicated work, most recently receiving the International Peace Award from the Reorganized Church of Jesus Christ of Latter Day Saints in 1998.

About the Contributors

Rachel Bundang was born in the Philippines and raised in the U.S. She is currently a Ph.D. candidate in Christian Ethics at Union Theological Seminary in New York City.

Mary E. Hunt is a feminist theologian and co-founder/co-director of The Women's Alliance for Theology, Ethics, and Ritual (WATER) in Silver Spring, MD. She is author of *Fierce Tenderness: A Feminist Theology of Friendship* published in 1990.

Andrea Smith is a member of the Cherokee Nation and a Ph.D. candidate in the History of Consciousness program at the University of California at Santa Cruz.

Traci C. West is Assistant Professor of Christian Ethics and African American Studies at Drew University Theological School. Her forthcoming book is *Wounds of the Spirit: Black Women, Violence, and Resistance Ethics.*

Introduction

Nantawan Boonprasat Lewis
Marie M. Fortune

Essays and a response to these essays in this volume represent a collaborative effort of the authors to address the issue of sexual violence against women from feminist/womanist theological perspectives. They are proceedings from a panel discussion presented by the authors under the theme "Remembering Conquest: Feminist/Womanist Perspectives on Religion, Colonization, and Sexual Violence" at the American Academy of Religion Annual Meeting in Orlando, Florida in 1998. We also wish to mention that the collaborative work on this panel to some major degree stemmed from a network of four women, white and of color, who participated in a conference on Violence Against Women in Toronto, Canada in the fall of 1996. This conference was sponsored by the Women's Desk of the World Council of Churches at whose request Marie Fortune and Thelma Burgonio-Watson of the Center for the Prevention of Domestic and Sexual Violence played a key role in organizing it with the Office of Justice for Women of the National Council of Churches and its counterpart in Canada.

Together, the four essays provide a multi-cultural, multi-racial and global analysis of sexual violence as experienced by women in various contexts under the United States' "colonial" rule and the role of religion as contributor to and source of liberation from this situation. Although the essays were coincidental to the centennial of the conquest of the United States over the Philippines in 1898, the essayists remind us that colonization has a far reaching and variegated impact

[Haworth co-indexing entry note]: "Introduction." Lewis, Nantawan Boonprasat, and Marie M. Fortune. Co-published simultaneously in *Journal of Religion & Abuse* (The Haworth Pastoral Press, an imprint of The Haworth Press, Inc.) Vol. 1, No. 2, 1999, pp. 1-4; and: *Remembering Conquest: Feminist/Womanist Perspectives on Religion, Colonization, and Sexual Violence* (ed: Nantawan Boonprasat Lewis and Marie M. Fortune) The Haworth Pastoral Press, an imprint of The Haworth Press, Inc., 1999, pp. 1-4. Single or multiple copies of this article are available for a fee from The Haworth Document Delivery Service [1-800-342-9678, 9:00 a.m. - 5:00 p.m. (EST). E-mail address: getinfo@haworthpressinc.com].

on women and their societies that is extended to the present time. It will unquestionably continue to have devastating consequences on their lives if this domination and oppression supported and enforced by other oppressive forces goes unchallenged. The essays, written from diverse experiences, strikingly share a view of the interconnection and intersection of patriarchy, colonialism, imperialism, racism, classism, capitalism and militarism which simultaneously and multi-facetedly contribute to violence against women. Regrettably, as pointed out by the authors, religions of the lands through their teaching and treatment of women have historically been a collaborating force of institutionalized exploitation and subordination of women. This results in the inferiority of woman and the use of her body at the will of an imperialistic, colonialistic, racist and patriarchal power. The essays pose a challenge to feminists/womanists in religion including religious communities: to persistently advocate for an embodiment of the spirit of resistance and liberation through working on creating counter interpretations of religion that point to its possibilities and promises to perform its task as a moral and ethical source for liberation of women and all her children and name the forces that attempt otherwise.

Nantawan Boonprasat Lewis focuses on a phenomenon of US colonization of Thailand in modern times and its relation to sexual violence against women which is expressed in a current form of the sex industry and the AIDS epidemic. She contends that Buddhism which is a dominant religion has been a source of moral ambiguity and liberation in this situation. Exploring Thai Buddhist feminists' responses to the phenomenon of the sex industry and AIDS in the context of global market economy, Lewis sees urgency for feminists/womanists in religion to embody their spirit of resistance. She feels a true need for a theological framework capable of addressing the situation that is at once personal, communal, national and global. This to her remains a critical challenge to the religious communities within and outside Thailand.

Speaking from Black American women's experience, Traci C. West views colonization as Afro-American internalization of Euro-American racism that presents a unique context to understand the relationship between Black and White. West then suggests that this type of relationship should be seen as "colonization of the mind" and as white supremacist psycho-social captivity of Black women which has yet to enter a post-colonial period. The rape of slaves provides a cultural-historical context to understand the rape of Black women today. Ultimately as West argues, white supremacist, sexist construction of Black women and Christian ideologies about women's innate guilt as victims of rape serves as a structural framework of the "occupied territory" in Black women's experience of sexual violence. In addressing sexual violence against Black women, one needs to be reminded of the historical connection between the church and European colonization. As West argues, the church itself must also be healed from this destructive logic of paternalistic conquest.

Andrea Smith's essay chronicles a horror history of violence done to American Indian women. As she documents and rigorously argues, sexual violence is not and should not be seen as part of American Indian tradition. Rather, it is a result of colonialism and racism generated by White Christian colonizers whose particular Biblical interpretation influenced their understanding of Indians as savages. Thus the Indians must be civilized, controlled and destroyed. Rape, murder and mutilation of Indian women's bodies were then justified. Such treatment of women provides a pattern of institutionalized violence and genocide of the Indian community and is internalized by some Indian men. This stigmatizes the community as being traditionally violent, an image that Smith's essay documents as untrue. Smith concludes that sexual violence, rape, and colonialism are interrelated. For efforts to address and end personal and state violence against Indian women to be successful, they must be done in an anti-colonial, anti-racist framework.

From a textbook case of colonization such as the Philippines, Rachel Bundang presents four provocative cases of Filipinas whose beings and experiences represent realities and scars of each historical period that the country was colonialized. The *Babaylan* (Tagalog, priestess), Maria Clara, Miss Saigon and Flor Contemplación are cases in point of how Filipinas' womanhood is closely intertwined and identified with her nationhood and its fate and destiny. Bundang offers ethics of right relation in place of dysfunctional relationship that the nation and the church have with women and calls on religion of the land to this revolutionary act.

It is critical that we understand the roots of colonialism, the ways in which sexual violence was and is used to promote and sustain it, and the intersection with religious doctrine, teaching and practice. These historical contexts are projected onto our contemporary experiences;

we all live with the heritage that history delivers to us. For those of us who are part of the dominant culture in North America, our understanding of these issues will increase our ability to participate as effective allies with those who bear the particular wounds and scars of contemporary sexual violence in a neo-colonial context.

We hope that the contribution of these four essays and the response from Mary E. Hunt will inspire readers to reflect critically on this timely and extraordinarily important issue and the challenge that it represents to religious communities in the United States and throughout the world.

We trust that these articles will encourage the reader to apply new insights to her/his setting of ministry or study.

Remembering Conquest:
Religion, Colonization and Sexual Violence:
A Thai Experience

Nantawan Boonprasat Lewis

SUMMARY. This essay limits itself to explore a particular experience–that of a Thai experience. It will focus on a phenomenon of US colonization of Thailand and its relation to sexual violence against women. The essay will assess Thai feminists' position on the role of religion as a source of moral ambiguity and liberation in this situation. It will suggest that a constructive solution to sexual violence against women in Thailand requires serious consideration of feminists' concerns and analysis of the situation as well as their proposal for reconstructing a new paradigm of right relations that takes seriously Thai women's history of struggle in a patriarchal culture. *[Article copies available for a fee from The Haworth Document Delivery Service: 1-800-342-9678. E-mail address: getinfo@haworthpressinc.com <Website: http://www.haworthpressinc.com>]*

KEYWORDS. Asian sex industry, Asian AIDS epidemic, Thai Buddhist feminism, Buddhism

INTRODUCTION

As we remember the centennial years of the US conquest over the Philippines, indigenous people, African Americans, Mexicans, etc., we are reminded that this colonization is not confined to the North American continent alone. Those in Asia and in other parts of the

---

[Haworth co-indexing entry note]: "Remembering Conquest: Religion, Colonization and Sexual Violence: A Thai Experience." Lewis, Nantawan Boonprasat. Co-published simultaneously in *Journal of Religion & Abuse* (The Haworth Pastoral Press, an imprint of The Haworth Press, Inc.) Vol. 1, No. 2, 1999, pp. 5-17; and: *Remembering Conquest: Feminist/Womanist Perspectives on Religion, Colonization, and Sexual Violence* (ed: Nantawan Boonprasat Lewis and Marie M. Fortune) The Haworth Pastoral Press, an imprint of The Haworth Press, Inc., 1999, pp. 5-17. Single or multiple copies of this article are available for a fee from The Haworth Document Delivery Service [1-800-342-9678, 9:00 a.m. - 5:00 p.m. (EST). E-mail address: getinfo@haworthpressinc.com].

5

world have lived through a colonized experience. Furthermore this essay wishes to remind us that the conquest is far from being "a thing of the past" but is a lived experience of many in the southern hemisphere. Only that current conquest has taken a new form and expression. Its social and political meanings however remain. The colonized lose control over their lives and find themselves in captivity, culturally, socially, economically and politically.

I shall begin with a recent personal experience which provided me with additional urgency to be part of solutions to this grievous situation. For years I have been working on the role of religion in relation to sex tourism in Asia and Thailand. Each trip that I made to Thailand during these two decades involved meetings with friends, colleagues and former students who work, teach and research on this topic to learn more about the current situation and to develop an analysis that reflects this reality. This led me to believe that I knew what was going on. However during this last trip which took place early in 1998, two events occurred at the beginning of my arrival which changed all assumptions.

THE KENLIAM EVENT

A few days after arriving in Bangkok, a friend called to inform me that there would be a panel discussion organized by the Women Foundation of Thailand and Global Alliance Against Traffic in Women on the topic "Who Will Help Thai Women's Labor Overseas?" at Rattanakosin Hotel in the heart of the Old Bangkok. I mention the name of this hotel because for those who might be familiar with the Thai Students' Movement in the 70s, this was the hotel to which students fled to escape from guns and bullets of the Thai military and police when they demanded the dictatorial Prime Minister and his cronies step down. This friend said I should go to hear the panel because it related to my subject of research. So I went and heard four panelists address cases of the plight of Thai women who were forced to work as slaves in a sweatshop in Elmonte, California and as prostitutes in Toronto, Canada and Japan. The moderator then introduced a panelist who was persuaded to go to France to be a domestic worker and discovered instead she was to work as a sexual service provider. She fortunately managed to escape and returned to Thailand. After an introduction from the moderator, we, the audience sat and waited eagerly to hear her story because other panelists were speaking from the experience of organizations which helped the women. Here was the chance for us to hear the victim's voice stating her case in front of representatives from the Office of Social Welfare, Ministry of Foreign Affairs, Police Department, NGOs, the Thai Press, women's groups, the UN Office of Refugee Affairs and Thai and foreign academics, etc.

Lawan Kenliam started her story with a sentence that she came from a very poor village in the Northeast of Thailand and was persuaded by a broker to go to work in France. When she arrived in France, she was told to sign a paper which identified her as a Laotian and was forced to work as a prostitute. Then she began to cry and was unable to say anything further. The audience and I sat in silence as we witnessed the pain of a woman who was invited to share with the public a very ugly and painful event in her life. And I cried with her.

THE CHIANG MAI EVENT

The week after that I went up north to Chiang Mai, the second largest city and one of the most visited tourist cities in the country. Due to the nature of my research I went to visit my former student who directs the Office of AIDS Ministry of the Church of Christ in Thailand to learn about his work in the region which has the highest percentage of the population being affected by AIDS. My student told me stories of AIDS patients and their struggles after learning that they were HIV positive, going through a full blown period of AIDS, coping with their resigned fate and contemplating on the future of their spouses and their children without them. I sat with him as he told and retold these stories and I cried.

More often than one likes to admit, tears represent an acknowledgment of a certain reality over which one has little or no control. They speak volumes of hurt, anguish and desperation one feels for being put in such a situation.

FROM VIETNAM WAR
TO THE INTERNATIONAL MONETARY FUNDS:
PROSTITUTION AS A NEW FORM OF COLONIZATION

These two emotional events, as different as they were, not surprisingly stem from a common phenomenon that is sweeping the country, the region and to a certain extent the world. It is a situation of societies under global capitalistic aggression and the horrific impacts this has on people's lives and in the Thai case on its women and their families. Many natives and expats have come to accept and admit that the US militaristic and economic expansion play a key role. This aggression, carried out under the name of Rest and Recreation for American soldiers during the Vietnam war, has gradually developed into a mega sex industry functioning within a new context of industrial globalization. Throughout, the abundant supply of "cheap-to-buy" women serves as an essential means of this aggression. As the number of women in the sex industry climbs to 2.8 million according to recent study,[1] prostitution becomes a new form of colonization in Thailand.

When women's sexuality is surrendered, the nation is more or less conquered!

Statistics speak for themselves. During the Vietnam War, there were at least five US military bases in the northeastern and eastern parts of Thailand. There were 40,000-50,000 GIs located on these bases. Between 1966-69, 30,000-70,000 American soldiers came to Thailand for R&R.[2] All kinds of entertainment businesses were created for this purpose–most important, the sex entertainment business. After the Vietnam War ended, there was a major campaign on tourism to sustain these entertainment businesses leading to the development of the sex industry. By the early 1990s, approximately six million tourists from the US, Europe, the Middle East and East Asia visited Thailand annually. The industry ranked as the third highest reliable source for foreign currency.[3] In 1995, this industry brought in $7.6 billion. As the number of tourists climbed to 7 million that same year, 65 percent were reportedly single men who were on vacations. Thai women played a key role in this export-led but invisible industry. The Thai economic miracle during the late 1980s to mid 1990s as several studies[4] point out was built on the bodies/backs of its own women.

As the First World and Thailand reaped the benefit and took pleasure from women's bodies, the AIDS epidemic emerged. When AIDS became news in the mid 1980s, it was first understood as a gay men's and foreigners' disease. But in an era when husband and wife must live apart as each seeks employment opportunities unavailable to them in their villages and hometown, there is a high rate of extramarital affairs with co-workers, prostitutes and acquaintances. At the end of the millennium, the spread of the disease was mostly due to prostitution and heterosexual relationships. It is estimated that 1.5 million Thais are HIV-infected. Two years ago, the Public Health Minister announced that an average of three people die of AIDS every two days (Thai Development Newsletter 1996). In addition, according to him, the HIV virus has penetrated nearly all villages in two northern provinces of Chaing Mai and Chaing Rai where five AIDS patients die everyday. In one district in Chiang Mai, the rate of AIDS-related deaths is higher than the birth rate. Seventy percent of AIDS patients nationwide are in an active laborforce group–between 15-24 years of age. Women now constituted 60% of the HIV infected population. According to the UNAIDs factsheet, an estimated 63,000 Thai children under the age of 15 are HIV infected and 47,000 will die of it by the year 2000. At the same time, 100,000 would have lost their mothers to the disease. One-third of these children would be less than 5 years old.[5]

NAMING INTERNAL AND RELATED FACTORS

Historians, social scientists, economists and political scientists recognize that the US militaristic and economic expansion, which began in the 1960s, led the path for colonizing Thailand and is perpetuated through global economy and industrial colonization. That trend reached its high point last year when economic crisis and the devaluation of the Baht led to the IMF bailout. As of early 1998, Thailand's economy is under complete control of the IMF. As recent as the fall of 1998 the NY Times reported that one thousand Thais lose jobs every day in addition to two million who were unemployed.

In spite of this significant external factor, there are to be sure several internal factors contributing to sexual violence against women in Thailand. Particularly, the failure of national economic and social development plans which have been introduced every five years since the year 1961. The focus of these plans includes the utilization of natural and human resources to expand the base of production, employment opportunities and national income. However, these plans failed to create an equitable distribution of economic wealth and growth and favor urban to rural development. This resulted in the bankruptcy of rural economic structures and a depletion of these resources to sustain the lives and well-being of its people. By the early 1970s the country began to witness a major migration of rural labor into big cities, especially those from the northeast and from certain parts of the north. And there were more women than men who migrated into cities. During the mid 1980s, Thailand shifted its emphasis in the national economic and social development plan from an agricultural based structure to promoting the country to become a newly industrialized nation (NICS) which relies heavily on western technology and capital goods to reach its goal. Sutheera Thompson's study indicates that 80-90% of the workforce in the industrial sector are women who are paid less than 50% of the minimum wage.[6] This latest development saw a brief success in the beginning of the 1990s when the country was showcased as an economic tiger in Asia along with Malaysia, Singapore, Taiwan, South Korea and Indonesia. Thailand was known as an emerging economy with a healthy annual growth rate of approximately 7% and an annual inflation rate under 5%. (In promoting more US investment in Thailand, Casper Wienburger once wrote in *Business Week* that Thailand represents one of the most stable economies in the region and is also the best friend the United States has in Southeast Asia.)

From late 1980s to mid 1990s the Thai economy was completely globalized. It was an export-oriented economy with at least five leading exporting industries, i.e., canned and frozen fish products, textiles, jewelry, footwear and knitware. Go to any department store in the US and look at label tags for a small surprise that many recognizable brand names, i.e., Levi's, Liz Claiborne, Anne Klien, Ralph Lauren, etc., all have their manufacturing plants in Thailand! What most economists fail to mention is that tourism has also become a major exporting industry in Thailand. And more important, the major tourist attractions are women who work in the sex entertainment business. This was a period known as "economic boom" with selective prosperities. In 1994, the regional income of people who live in the northeast of the country was estimated 10.2 times lower than those in Bangkok. In June 1997 Thailand declared its devaluation of the Baht and went through a period of currency crisis. In 1998, the country was completely under the control of the IMF and the World Bank. In a rather short period of time it has gone from a newly industrialized country to a newly economically colonized nation! What is still amazing is tourism is more than ever seen as a quick fix of this crisis. The Thai government launched a rigorous campaign to promote 1998 to be the year of Amazing Thailand. But as correctly assessed by Bishop and

Robinson, "If tourism is to be as central to Thailand's economic recovery as it was to the kingdom's boom-time development–and it can hardly be otherwise, since the planned bailout entails no new industrial or agricultural directions–sex will continue to be essential to tourism and hence to the nation's economic rescue. Thailand's 'miracle' was built on the backs of women working on their backs; the reconstruction process will doubtless make use of the same means."[7]

THE OTHER SIDE OF THE STORY

Several studies point out that at the heart of the struggle of Thai women is the male-female relationship, that is a relationship of subordination which is institutionalized in the social, economic, political, and cultural structure of the country with religion as the source of meaning and legitimization. Historically, religion has provided both moral ambiguity and a source of liberation for the struggle of women.[8]

In explaining why there is such tolerance concerning the sex trade, which is an overt form of sexual violence against women, both Thai and expatriate feminist scholars agree on the following factors, namely the lack of control of women's bodies as revealed throughout Thai history and as practiced within the family institution, a religious view of women as body, an image of women as mother, wife and whore which is related to women's right to define gender relations in Thai society, and last but not least a popular interpretation of the law of karma. All these will be succinctly discussed below.

From its early days, Thai patriarchal society viewed women as property–of parents, husband or men in general. This led to unequal power relations between men and women. During feudalistic society, slaves were bought and traded among lords. Children were considered the property of parents and a wife of her husband. Thus they could be bought or traded at their parents' or husband's will. Under this social system, men were considered the head of the household. A woman's status depended on the status of her men who generally belonged to a particular lord. When the country was changed into a monarchical democratic system, the right to one's own life and property was improved. But because of lack of education, vocational skills and opportunities, women are still viewed as inferior to men. Chit Phumisak, a known Thai Marxist scholar, noted that the Thai feudalistic system defined women as sex objects and loyal slaves. According to him, evidences of this attitude were many in Thai classical literature and historical documents, i.e., Ramayana Epic, Phra Apai Manee, the Three Seals Code of 1805, etc. All view women as sex objects and part of men's wealth and fame.[9] Under a global capitalist economy where Thai society has gone through enormous changes, the Thai patriarchal value remains intact and women are still viewed as sex machines.

In popular Thai Buddhism, women clearly hold a lower status than men. They were not allowed to be ordained into monkhood. Yet as pointed out by noted anthropologists Charles Keyes and Thomas Kirsch, women play a key role as material providers to the religion. A Thai Buddhist culture of gender, Keyes opines, projects the dominant image of women as mother or nurturer whose role is not confined to just within her family but as nurturer of the Buddhist institutions–by providing her sons to become monks and through routine merit-making activities. Their sex roles create a cultural expectation of women to be in charge of the family purse string and petty marketing while men enjoy a position of authority in religious, political and social worlds.

Sukanya Harntrakul, a famous Thai feminist journalist, observes that in Thai feudalism where the family institution was closedly linked with political and governmental structure, women's bodies and their sexual relations with men were the means for economic survival of society and for family well-being and survival. There were good women whose dominant role was of mother and prostitutes whose main role was purely sexual. Both however were dependent on men. These two aspects of women's existence were seen as two sides of the same coin where men remain at the center providing meaning to their being socially and economically. In this context, Harntrakul points out, women only have two options, that of being mother or prostitute. Thus it is understandable that Thai women were transformed from being wives (as defined by the Three Seal Code of 1805, which classified women into three categories: the principle wife whose marriage met with the consent of parents, the secondary wife who was favored by the husband, and the slave wife who came through debt bondage or other political arrangement) into the status of principle wife, minor wife and rented wife during the 1960s and 70s, to masseuses, prostitutes, Ago-Go Girls, call girls, escorts, waitresses in Karaoke and arranged-marriage wives who are later sold to pimps in foreign countries in the 1990s. As a whole this transformation of women's status which is based on their sexual relations with men reflects the social and cultural control of women's sexuality. In early Thai history royal women were used as pawns to save the country from being colonized by a foreign power. In contemporary Thailand, rural and poor women's bodies were sold in exchange for the economic security of families, communities and society as a whole. Thus Ryan Bishop and Lilian Robinson's famous words, "the Thai economic miracle is built on the backs of women; the reconstruction process will doubtless make use of the same means."[10]

Among women in prostitution and their families a popular interpretation of the Buddhist law of karma is instrumental in their acceptance of injustices against them. Their response to an inquiry why they do what they do frequently ends up with the law of karma. According to this interpretation of karma, one enjoys prosperities and happiness in this life because of the good deeds and merits one accumulated during previous lives. Suffering and bad things happen in this life because of insufficient merits from previous lives. This also applies to being born as a woman, being poor, having low social status and other bad happenings. The powerful law of karma interpreted this way conditions one's understanding of gender, wealth, power and social status. As pointed out by Suwanna Satha-Anand, this explanation suggests and enforces the traditional Thai society's view and treatment of women as subordinate to men. In her words,

> Once this line of reasoning is accepted, it is only "natural" that women occupy an inferior status in this life. This should not be understood that being born a female is permanent to a person's nature. It applies only in this life. There are always opportunities to change one's sexual fate. What one can do is to "make and store" one's merit in this life so that one will be reborn a male in the next.[11]

Satha-Anand continues to challenge this thought in stating that "The fact that one's sexuality is actually not permanent seems to reinforce the power of the Buddhist's belief in women's inferiority." She concludes; "This is because Buddhism has offered a way out within the system, and in 'working that way out,' women are in effect strengthening the belief in their inferiority. If sexuality was seen as fixed (as there would probably be no next rounds of rebirths), necessity for immediate revolt against the system might have been more viable."[12]

RELIGION AS LIBERATION:
TOWARDS THAI FEMINIST THEOLOGY OF LIBERATION

In the midst of the economic and health crisis under aggression of a global capitalistic and patriarchal system, it is gratifying to see recognition of male scholars, both native and expat, speaking in support of female agency. In concluding his article entitled "Thailand's Economic Miracle: Built on the Backs of Women," where he advocates for the end of capitalistic patriarchy that exploits Thai women, Peter Bell acknowledges that "women are at the cutting edge of the struggle in Thailand."[13] There are evidences that Thai feminist theologians, both Buddhist and Christian, have taken the task as well. There are at least two Buddhist feminist approaches on this matter representing an understanding that religion can be a source of solutions to prostitution, AIDS, and colonization in Thailand by addressing the man-woman relationship of subordination.

AN APOLOGETIC VIEW:
A RETURN TO THE ORIGINAL TEACHING OF BUDDHISM

Buddhist feminist theologian Chatsumarn Kabilsingh, for example, views the teaching of the Buddha as helpful to the problem of prostitution. There were prostitutes during the time of Buddha who took refuge in his teaching and finally gave up the profession and became female monks. The Buddha himself accepted all human beings, male and female as being equal in their spiritual attainment. If prostitutes turn to the Four Noble Truths of the Buddha and begin to understand their suffering, they too can improve their fate and realize the highest truth. They then will not place value in physical and sensual experience that only lead to greater suffering. Kabilsingh's position reflects her attempt to address one of the internal factors causing women to go into the sex business and be exploited, namely materialism.

However, her apologetic view is not without a critical assessment of the role of the Sangha (the body of monkhood). Monks are held in high esteem in Thai society as representatives of the Buddha in terms of providing spiritual guidance to lay believers. In return the laity provide the material needs of monks. The monk-laity relationship is considered mutual in this way. Regrettably, there are cases of monks who view women as inferior to men and teach the evil karma of prostitutes. These monks encourage women in prostitution to give more material support to the temples in order to accumulate more merits for the next life leading them to justify their plight and undermining the true causes of the situation. Kabilsingh thus advocates for the Sangha to be more involved in providing spiritual guidance to the laity and to deal with their own fear of having women being equal to men. The social crisis, she says, is greater than this fear and needs the cooperation and involvement of all, regardless of gender, class and ethnicity.[14]

CULTURAL EMPOWERING OF WOMEN: FEMINIST ANALYSIS AND RE-INTERPRETATION OF THE SACRED TEXT

Although in agreement with Kabilsingh in viewing religion as a liberating source for the struggle of women in Thailand, Suwanna Satha-Anand proposes to address the relationship of subordination by advocating for cultural empowering of women. In her view, there are at least two approaches to address the situation, namely the structural and situational.

By structural approach, Satha-Anand means

> A concerted effort to be made to re-direct or re-orient the economic development policy–particularly the development of women. This approach includes attempts in changing unfair family laws, better law enforcement, as well as re-reading and re-interpretation of certain elements in traditional and religious cultures which have been putting women in subordinate positions for so long.[15]

The situational approach is intended to address specific programs and actions that would help women in their particular case and circumstance, i.e., providing more alternative vocational skills, extending literacy education, and knowledge about law and rights, etc. Her focus is however on the structural approach by specifically addressing cultural empowering of women through "injecting feminist perspective" into key passages of the Buddhist Tripitaka and tales and feminist analysis of the Vessantara jataka tale. By reinterpreting such texts to affirm women's equal relationship with men, to critically analyze why women cannot be the Buddha, and pointing out the cultural and historical condition of the time when the text was written, she believes "would put an end to the monopoly of highest spiritual attainment of the male members of the Thai society" and help to transform the cultural and traditional value of women as subordinate to men. In doing so, one can eliminate a so-called push factor of prostitution.

Both Kabilsingh and Satha-Anand's theological attempts are commendable efforts to address what is understood to be a foundational element/cause of sexual violence against women as expressed in the case of prostitution in the Thai sex industry. Although differing in their approaches and analytical methods, both challenge the Thai cultural understanding and social treatment of women. A question remains whether the injustices and exploitation of Thai women in its current form can afford to be viewed within a personal, communal and national structural framework. As this paper discusses, such injustices to a large extent result from global power arrangements and global power relations that put women at the bottom, and are complicated by her class, race, ethnicity, religion and cultural differences. If the root cause of the problem is about (unjust) relationships and (unequal) power relations, an approach needed seems to be one that addresses the complexity and multiplicity of the situation, including the power relations of the male-female relationship. This is because what needs to be transformed is not just the male-female relations, but the power relations that are interconnected, intersected and operated on a cosmic scale. A close look at Thailand is just a case in point.

NOTES

1. Peter Bell, ."Thailand's Economic Miracle Built on the Backs of Women," *Women, Gender Relations and Development in Thai Society*, eds. Virada Somswasdi & Sally Theobald, I (Chiang Mai: Women Studies Center, Chiang Mai University, 1997), 68.

2. Teeranart Karnjanaaksorn, "Problem and Socio-Economic Conditions Impacting on Trade on Women," *Journal of Social Research* 14:2 (1991) in Thai.

3. Thai Development Newsletter, 20 (1991/1992), 15.

4. See footnotes no. 1. and 2. See also Ryan Bishop and Lillian S. Robinson, *Night Market: Sexual Culture and the Thai Economic Miracle* (New York: Routledge, 1998).

5. *Thai Development Newsletter*, 31 (1996), 15.

6. Ngaosinn Kongkaew, "Career Decision That Rural Thai Women Must Accept," *Women and The Changing Power*, ed. Kobkul Ingudananda (Bangkok: Kobfai, 1994) in Thai.

7. Bishop & Robinson, op. cit., 251.

8. See, for example, Sukanya Harntrakul, "Democracy: Distribution of Sexual Power," *Women and the Changing Power*, ed. Kobkul Ingudananda (Bangkok: Kobfai, 1994) in Thai; Sucheela Tanchainan, *Women in Chit Pumisak's View* (Bangkok: Pluk, 1997) in Thai; Chatsuman Kabinsingh, *Thai Women in Thai Buddhism* (Berkeley (CA): Parallex Press, 1991).

9. Tanchainan, op. cit.

10. Bishop & Robinson, op. cit., 251.

11. Suwanna Satha-Anand, "Thai Prostitution, Buddhism and 'New Rights' in Southeast Asia," paper presented for the workshop on New Issues in East Asian Human Rights, Seoul, Korea, October 2-5, 1996, 6.

12. Ibid.

13. Bell, op. cit., 72.

14. Kabilsingh, *Thai Women in Buddhism*.

15. Satha-Annand, op. cit., 13.

16. Ibid, 20.

Spirit-Colonizing Violations:
Racism, Sexual Violence
and Black American Women

Traci C. West

SUMMARY. One way to recognize the imprint of racism in black women's experience of sexual violence is to identify its "colonizing" effect, that is, its attempt to occupy their minds, bodies and spirits, to claim them as objects to be defined and controlled by external, subjugating forces. To clarify the relevance of this understanding of colonization for contemporary instances of sexual violence we must first locate its meaning in the historical context and experiences of black American women. This contextualization allows us to apply a notion of colonization that is rooted in a recognizable past and repels its usage as a disembodied, universalizing metaphor. Then, specific, current examples from women's lives enable us to glimpse how "colonizing" dynamics produce a racist intensification of their anguish in the aftermath of sexual violence. Finally, an analytical emphasis on colonization also guides us toward a few cautions about organizing resistance to this combined social and sexual violence. It yields insight into how "colonizing" features of racism can saturate even Christian feminist responses to the violence. *[Article copies available for a fee from The Haworth Document Delivery Service: 1-800-342-9678. E-mail address: getinfo@haworthpressinc.com <Website: http://www.haworth pressinc.com>]*

KEYWORDS. African-American women, racism, sexual violence, colonization

[Haworth co-indexing entry note]: "Spirit-Colonizing Violations: Racism, Sexual Violence and Black American Women." West, Traci C. Co-published simultaneously in *Journal of Religion & Abuse* (The Haworth Pastoral Press, an imprint of The Haworth Press, Inc.) Vol. 1, No. 2, 1999, pp. 19-30; and: *Remembering Conquest: Feminist/Womanist Perspectives on Religion, Colonization, and Sexual Violence* (ed: Nantawan Boonprasat Lewis and Marie M. Fortune) The Haworth Pastoral Press, an imprint of The Haworth Press, Inc., 1999, pp. 19-30. Single or multiple copies of this article are available for a fee from The Haworth Document Delivery Service [1-800-342-9678, 9:00 a.m. - 5:00 p.m. (EST). E-mail address: getinfo@haworthpressinc.com].

19

"LOCATING" COLONIZATION
AS A MEANINGFUL CATEGORY

In several ways, a colonization paradigm does not fit the experience of black Americans. Black Americans are not comprised of indigenous peoples who remain on the land of their ancient ancestors after surviving a history of having been invaded, occupied, displaced and "conquered" by European colonists. As is well known, black Americans are the product of the European slave trade. They are often referred to as Diaspora people whose history includes African ancestors that were kidnapped or bought, removed from their land and homes, taken to another continent, and owned as pieces of property. There are distinctive legacies of this slave experience that bear concrete historical meaning for black American identity and differ from the legacies and impacts facing descendants of colonized peoples.

However, in its attempt to accurately reflect an historical consciousness, the use of the label "Diaspora people" fails to capture the rootedness of black Americans in the United States. Starting from its earliest history, they have played fundamental cultural, political and economic roles in building this nation. Black involuntary labor was essential to creating U.S. wealth and independence from the early seventeenth century onward. In the ante-bellum period, black women were laborers in the fields and the masters' homes, and they functioned as the producers of the country's primary capital (slaves). In the "peculiar institution" of U.S. slavery, the ongoing close proximity of slave owners and slaves in their living conditions not only inculcated the frequent "habit" of sexual violence by slave masters, but also created an intertwined cultural relationship between whites and blacks that permanently altered American society.

Moreover, the experiences of free blacks particularly evidence the need to historically demarcate our analytical use of the term "colonization." Certain free blacks voluntarily fought in the war for independence against the British, helped to displace the Indians in what U.S. Americans called the "westward expansion" of this nation, and created some thriving communities even including Literary Societies (e.g., in 1830s Boston and Philadelphia). Throughout the United States' past there hardly exists an aspect of political, social or economic "American identity" that does not include the significant participation of blacks. Thus a colonization paradigm is most relevant for describing Afro-American internalization of Euro-American racism. It is an invalid, misleading tool of inquiry insofar as it would encourage anyone to assume an "us vs. them" colonial relationship between blacks and a foreign nation called the United States of America, or imply the possibility of a U.S. colonized identity that can be isolated from blacks' indigenous identity. Afro-Americans have a United States indigenous identity. Ironically, the complexity of this identity is similar to the context in which some women who have been sexually assaulted by an intimate family member can find themselves. Often she and her abuser have jointly helped to shape their family culture as well as significantly contributed to each other's psychic identity. Thus, an intimate link, a "family tie" is forged, that binds them even though it incorporates cruel and dehumanizing elements for the woman.

It is in another kind of link between the concept of colonization and Euro-American racism that substantial insight is indeed offered for probing existing conditions for black Americans, like the consequences of male rape for black women. There are common elements between the peculiar racist logic of European colonizers and European slavers (who transmitted this logic to their progeny–Euro-Americans). For Afro-Americans, Euro-American racism can be understood as having attempted and largely achieved a type of "colonization of the mind." This type of white racist "occupation" that blacks experience indeed bears some identical markings to the literal occupation and post-colonial experience of indigenous peoples around the world living in the aftermath of European "conquest."

This historical sensitivity for applying the term colonialism to the psycho-social conditions of black women helps us to avoid the construction of a completely non-materialist, transhistorical notion of colonialism and post-colonialism. With regard to post-colonialism, I admit to broad suspicions about its current existence. These suspicions include my emphasis upon conceptualizing the colonization of blacks as white supremacist psycho-social captivity, as well as my claims about the importance of differentiating the actual historical and material conditions of third world peoples who were colonized by Europeans from the legacies of U.S. slavery. In both cases I am quite dubious about any assumption that we have even entered a post-colonial period.

Of course the common practice of culturally sanctioned rape that black women slaves faced is not so different from the history of indigenous women who lived under colonial rule. Slave rapes are a specific expression of Euro-American racism that bequeaths a complex legacy for our cultural understanding of the rape of black women today. This practice began from the journey on slave ships and continued in slave women's lives through "breeding" practices as well as in the incidental access of masters to slave women. As Linda Brent (a.k.a. Harriet Jacobs) commented, usually from the age of twelve a slave girl will soon "learn to tremble when she hears her master's footfall. . . . That which commands admiration in the white woman only hastens the degradation of the female slave . . . My master met me at every turn, reminding me that I belonged to him, and swearing that he would compel me to submit to him."[1] If we were to engage in a gynocentric chronicling of the brutalities of racism in United States history (a perspective that is rarely offered), we would have to name rape as a central ingredient. That the rape of black women has been such an important historical manifestation in the expression of white supremacy in the United States suggests the inadequacy of investigating racism without attention to rape or rape without attention to white supremacy.

This slave legacy means that, unlike that of Euro-American women, the history of rape against Afro-American women is not a secret history. Even many school children learn to articulate as fact the common knowledge that slave masters sometimes whipped and raped black slave women. Therefore, that black women have been raped, or that they are rapable based upon their intrinsic identity as black women is "known," public moral knowledge in our society.

RACIST INTENSIFICATION OF WOMEN'S ANGUISH

In their experience of rape, as in the rest of their life negotiations, racial, gender, sexual and spiritual identity issues overlap for black women. These categories are never distinct from one another but are, in my favorite terminology of feminist theorist Judith Butler, imbricated modalities.[2] Even in this discussion of rape, when the focus is upon racist patterns that influence identity, or on how these racist patterns may parallel and fuse with gendered social constructions, one should not deduce that racial and gender social identities are at any point truly isolated from one another. In the consciousness and lived experiences of women's lives, these dynamics are continuously implicated within one another.

Let us center our attention on self-blame, an aspect of shame that women who have been sexually assaulted may experience.[3] This is only one element in the emotional and spiritual consequences that can impact women victim-survivors. Sometimes it is the perpetrator himself who induces self-blame in a woman. He may indicate to the woman he victimizes that she is a willing partner in the violence. As a result, she may come to feel that she is somehow responsible for the crime.

Charlotte Pierce-Baker who was raped by two strangers in her own home while her husband and child were present, describes how this problem surfaced for her. After the rape, she was haunted by the way the rapist had told her to keep silent about the crime. He had whispered: "you don't want your husband to know what you have been doing down here, do you?" She replied: "no." At the time, she and the rapist were in the living room and her husband was confined upstairs. Reflecting on this exchange later, Pierce-Baker comments: "Perhaps the secrets began there, with my assuming responsibility for the horror he was perpetrating on me."[4] She explains how her concerns about the need to maintain secrecy are partly related to a sense of racial responsibility. Because the rapists were black men, she says, "I had to keep the rape secret–I had a responsibility. But to whom? For what? Almost as if the crime had been perpetrated by someone I trusted."[5]

The pressures that Pierce-Baker poignantly describes might be understood in the following way. White supremacy marginalizes blacks. The fact that they are part of this same marginalized group establishes a kind of kinship between her and the perpetrators. Their "kinship" as targets of white supremacist elements of American culture, simulates a communal bond. Anguishingly for a woman in this situation, it includes an allegiance to, and alliance with, the men who assaulted her. Though it is in fact, a treacherous one for her, this bond creates the specter of her collusion with the men. Thus, both the perpetrator's words and a sense that she perhaps owes these "brothers" something, reinforce her culpability in the crime committed against her, and press her to be silent and keep it secret.

Sometimes self-blame is related to discrediting, popular ideas about what it means to be an "authentic victim." Women who have been raped as children often report that the perpetrator told them somehow invited or wanted the abuse. Frequently, affection alternates with violence in the context of a long-term abusive relationship, such as in situations of childhood sexual abuse or marital rape. These contradictory dynamics can make women's perceptions of themselves as "true victims" come into question. Women may decide that if they do not exclusively feel disgust and anger toward their abusers, they share part of the blame for the assault. For some, self-blame can surface because they may not have experienced every moment of the actual assault as brutal.

For instance, incest survivor/author Melba Wilson describes how her feelings of self-blame made her fearful about speaking out about her abuse. They convey some of the particular racial/gender issues with which she must contend. Wilson was sexually abused by her father for several months when she was about twelve years old. As an adult writing about incest she shares her own experience and bravely admits: "I was afraid . . . that the physical pleasure which, if I was honest, I have to admit was part of it, meant that if I looked too closely at myself and the incest, I would somehow find that the stereotype of loose sexual morality might after all apply to me."[6] Fortunately, the burden of struggling with such stereotypes did not succeed in persuading her that because she was morally blameworthy she had to keep quiet. But, this social assault is still unrelenting for women.

White supremacist and sexist constructions of black women as prone to sexual promiscuity are publicly "confirmed" or alluded to in many ways, including recently by social policy "experts" and politicians during the 1995 welfare reform hearings. Such public moral indictments merge with the discrediting social invention of an "authentic" or "innocent" sexual assault victim. Together, these cultural messages help produce in women the kind of racial/gendered self-blame that Wilson describes. As she decides whether or not to reveal her experience of sexual assault these emotionally and spiritually debilitating dynamics conjoin, opposing and invalidating her own knowledge of herself as victim.

Black women victim-survivors can find themselves held innately responsible for their racial subjugation in a fashion that mirrors and complements the self-blame induced by their experience of male violence. Frantz Fanon's commentary on the psychology of colonization, particularly in *Black Skin, White Masks* usefully reveals the dynamics of the inferiority complex that white supremacist subjugation can weave into the consciousness of black people.[7] In engaging his ideas on the psychology of colonization to further our understanding of black women's trauma after sexual assault, I acknowledge that for Fanon, as bell hooks writes, "not only is the female body, black or white, always a sexualized body, always not the body that 'thinks,' but it also appears to be a body that never longs for freedom."[8] Yet, I do not hesitate to adapt Fanon's theories for this feminist analysis of sexual violence. As hooks would agree, we can still learn from sexist male theorists and we have certainly not severed our intellectual reliance on and deference to European and white American ones.[9]

As Fanon helps us to perceive, since whites are the standard by which blacks are measured, the black person perpetually suffers "from not being white." This white standard, he explains, imposes "discrimination on me, makes me a colonized native, robs me of all worth, all individuality, tells me that I am a parasite on the world . . . "[10] Throughout his work, Fanon emphasizes that this task of convincing blacks of their cultural inferiority is essential to white domination.

White domination nurtures and reinforces self-blame in blacks. In the United States, it is expressed in terms of cultural marginalization and (for most) economic disenfranchisement, and works to convince blacks of their parasitic role in society. We are repeatedly taught that Europeans and Euro-Americans–that is, white people, not African Americans, are the agents and subjects of history. To be convinced that in relation to the rest of the world one has not made any valuable contribution, but exists mainly as a burdensome dependent, makes one's subjugation seem rational. If one accepts these prevailing determinants of status and worth as just, the inevitable failure and accompanying sense of shame appear to be deserved. The presumption of black inferiority provides a rational basis for blacks to affix blame to themselves for any social barriers that they encounter and cannot surmount. It validates any cultural inadequacy that they experience.

The kinds of prevailing norms that illustrate this concept assume that status and privilege in our society are conferred upon those who deserve it, even minor, "everyday" forms of it, such as being positively recognized by any stranger who sees you arriving at high school with books under your arms as appearing to be a normal "all-American" teenager, or having city taxis unhesitatingly stop for you. And, in terms of cultural standards, it is assumed that classical ("high culture") music and arts are European or Euro-American in origin, as are the most theoretically sophisticated and foundational intellectual ideas and principles.

Fanon scholar Hussein Abdilahi Bulhan describes how as a result of the combined impact of racial myths about blacks and the evident structure of white dominance, the black person can be consigned to feelings of shame and guilt over her body and whole race.[11] Bulhan explains that often there "is not only a rejection of one's body and self, but also a verdict of eternal guilt."[12] Fanon metaphorically describes this condition: "I am guilty. I do not know of what, but I know that I am no good."[13] Under the existing conditions of white domination, where whites are the standard by which blacks are measured, blacks are perpetually guilty of not being white. This can make inferior status and self-blame for that inferior status inescapable for them.

Racial messages about innate guilt merge with gendered messages such as ideas about women's bodies (and often even those of little girls) as innately inviting of sexual attention from men, so: men "just can't help" but respond to that invitation. Christian biblical lessons about women's devious seductive powers can also combine with these ideas to reinforce our belief in women's tendency to deliberately use their "sexual powers" to morally corrupt men like Eve did. Racially based self-blaming assertions can form a destructive partnership with Christian traditions that teach us that women cry rape or attempted rape to punish men, like Potiphar's wife did to Joseph when he refused her explicit invitation to have sex with him.

These cultural constructions are so similar to self-blaming messages attached to a woman's sexual assault experience, that they can be understood as collaboratively helping to prove her culpability in her rape. In other words, these white supremacist, sexist and Christian ideologies about her innate guilt represent a spiritual assault that can be understood as already "occupying" her identity. Hence, when a woman is sexually assaulted, the words and attitude of her abuser, a family member, a police officer or a clergy member, that blame her, can fit snugly and devastatingly into that "occupied territory" of her racial and gender blameworthiness.

DE-COLONIZING CHRISTIAN RESPONSES TO WOMEN

We should not only be concerned about particular woman-blaming Christian traditions that can participate in the colonizing impact of sexual violence for black women. But, the problematic heritage of Christian involvement in earlier forms of European colonialism may continue to be present in, and undermining of, otherwise well-meaning, organized Christian efforts to address sexual violence. Churches have tremendous potential for supporting women, confronting abusers, and developing preventative strategies for every age-group. Currently, many church attempts to include violence against women on their agendas are relegated to mission committees or organized as mission out-reach programs. Unfortunately, it is also in this same area of Christian missions that an intense historical connection between the church and European colonization can be found.

Christianity played an active partnership role in the launching of European colonization throughout the world. These efforts especially flourished during the 16th, 17th, and 18th centuries. The goals of European colonization and European Christianity shared basic assumptions about the need to "conquer" the natives they encountered. Though state claims focused upon conquering their territory, while the expressed interest of the church was on "conquering" their souls, both understood themselves as fulfilling the mission of extending the boundaries of "civilization."

As Lott Carey, a black Baptist missionary (born a slave) declared in 1820 when he set off to begin his missionary life in Africa: "I long to preach to the poor Africans the way of life and salvation. I don't [sic] know what may befal [sic] me, or whether I may find a grave in the ocean, or among the savage men, or more savage wild beasts . . . "[14] Although a black American missionary is not at all representative of the participants in the vast Christian missionary movement that invaded Africa, Asia and the Americas for several centuries, the attitude that Lott expresses here certainly is typical. This zealous point of view about Christian salvation is at best paternalistic. In many ways, it represents an outright dehumanization of the natives who are seen as only slightly more tame than the beasts of the African jungle. Most important to this discussion, it constitutes a disturbing legacy of objectifying those being "saved."

Vestiges of this paternalistic approach may remain in contemporary state and church sponsored outreach efforts. There continues to be a paternalistic ideological partnership between certain aspects of Christianity and the arm of the State when they make funding available to or develop projects centered upon helping "people with problems," such as women who have been raped. Organized efforts dependent upon state and/or church resources may reflect the colonizing/missionary values of their sponsors by actively helping to construct women who have been raped as problematized "others," that is, where the woman and "her problems" are seen as the object of our mission to help.

In attempts to provide services to those victimized by sexual assault there is often an implicit assumption that the service-provider reaches out to help the woman to become well or to "heal." While this naturally seems like a supportive gesture, it may also reinforce a perception that there is something wrong with the woman, rather than with the perpetrator and sexual assault itself. To construct responses to sexual violence that are solely focused upon healing the woman might be to participate in an effort that is too thoroughly focussed upon pursuing the goal of "managing rape" rather than "stopping the violence" as Nancy Matthews terms it in *Confronting Rape: The Feminist Anti-Rape Movement and the State*.[15]

Moreover, when we create the impression that a particular bureaucratic response concentrating on the issue of the sexual assault incident(s) can offer women a "safe space" where women can "heal," a deception is perpetrated. Of course the space created in the church, the pastoral counselor's office or the therapy group, is neither safe nor able to produce healing from the ongoing assault that white supremacy represents in black women's lives. This claim advertises a post-colonial sanctuary where one cannot possibly exist. In fact, such a claim may only unwittingly reiterate to a woman that she is indeed a burdensome dependent on the world, who needs to be offered a place to be fixed.

If the colonizing/missionary logic of organized anti-violence efforts is not explicitly challenged, a woman victim-survivor may find herself in a familiar trap. She may find Christian outreach projects and counseling to be like her indigenous United States cultural identity where she is both principle contributor and outsider, and her racial kinship to black male perpetrators, whether strangers or actual family members, that is laced with treachery. A destructive paternalism is included as the church reaches out to her, claiming her as sister. That these similar social and religious messages are so consistent with her wrenching experience of sexual assault may confirm for her that it is simply part of the natural course of life that black women suffer.

To disrupt this pattern requires a de-colonizing of our collective spirits. It can happen, in part, by maintaining a religious emphasis on an anti-racist, public sphere movement to end sexual violence that occurs in places like church school classrooms, in front of city halls, on opinion-editorial pages of newspapers. This emphasis helps to reject the rooting of "the problem" in a black woman's selfhood, relocating it in the perpetrator's choices and our societal inadequacies that support his choices. It means honoring her right to freedom and dignity of mind, body and spirit as we work side by side to challenge the intimate and social assaults.

NOTES

1. *Linda Brent, Incidents in the Life of a Slave Girl*, edited by L. Maria Child, New Introduction and Notes by Walter Teller (New York: Harcourt, Brace, Jovanovich, 1973), 26-28.

2. Judith Butler, *Bodies That Matter: On the Discursive Limits of "Sex"* (New York: Routledge, 1993).

3. Several of my ideas about race, gender and self-blame discussed in this section of the essay are further developed and expanded in my book *Wounds of the Spirit: Black Women, Violence and Resistance Ethics* (New York: New York University Press, 1999).

4. Charlotte Pierce-Baker, *Surviving the Silence: Black Women's Stories of Rape* (New York: W.W. Norton, 1998), 64.

5. Pierce-Baker, 63.

6. Melba Wilson, *Crossing the Boundary: Black Women Survive Incest*, 89.

7. Frantz, Fanon, *Black Skin, White Masks*, Charles Markmann, trans. (New York: Grove Press, 1967). Although Fanon's work focuses on black people in the Caribbean and North Africa, his theoretical framework for describing cultural, political and economic domination by whites of European ancestry applies to current psychosocial conditions for black Americans.

8. bell hooks, "Feminism as a Persistent Critique of History: What's Love Got to Do with It?" in Alan Read ed., *The Fact of Blackness: Frantz Fanon and Visual Representation* (Seattle: Bay Press, 1996), 84.

9. See hooks' discussion of this point where she discusses white feminist zealousness to discard sexist black male writers while they would never even imagine excluding Shakespeare or Joyce from their reading lists or suppose that one could overlook Derrida or Jameson. bell hooks, *Yearning: Race, Gender, and Cultural Politics* (Boston: South End Press, 1990) especially her essay, "Representations: Feminism and Black Masculinity."

10. Fanon, *Black Skin, White Masks*, 139.

11. Bulhan, Hussein Abdilahi, *Frantz Fanon and the Psychology of Oppression* (New York: Plenum Press, 1985).

12. Bulhan, Hussein Abdilahi, 192.

13. Fanon, *Black Skin, White Masks*, 139.

14. As quoted in Sandy Dwayne Martin, "Black Baptists, Foreign Missions, and African Colonization, 1814-1882," in Sylvia M. Jacobs, ed., *Black Americans and the Missionary Movement in Africa* (Westport, CT: Greenwood Press, 1982) 51.

15. Nancy Matthews, *Confronting Rape: The Feminist Anti-Rape Movement and the State* (New York: Routledge, 1994).

Sexual Violence
and American Indian Genocide

Andrea Smith

SUMMARY. This paper discusses the relationship between Christian imperialism, colonialism and sexual violence within Native communities. It is inadequate to conceptualize sexual violence simply as a tool of patriarchy, because sexual violence has served as a primary tool of racism and genocide against Native peoples. Thus, colonialism and sexual violence cannot be separated. This relationship also compels anti-violence advocates to develop responses to sexual violence that do not at the same time strengthen institutions of colonialism and racism. *[Article copies available for a fee from The Haworth Document Delivery Service: 1-800-342-9678. E-mail address: getinfo@haworthpressinc.com <Website: http://www.haworthpressinc.com>]*

KEYWORDS. Christianity, colonialism, genocide, sexual violence, American Indian

I once attended a conference where a speaker stressed the importance of addressing sexual violence within Native communities. When I returned home, I told a friend of mine, who was a rape survivor, about the speaker's talk. She replied, "You mean other Indian women have been raped?" When I said yes, she asked, "Well, why don't we ever talk about it?" Indeed, the silence surrounding sexual violence in Native communities–particularly the sexual assault of adult women–is overwhelming. Under Janet Reno, the Department of Justice has poured

---

[Haworth co-indexing entry note]: "Sexual Violence and American Indian Genocide." Smith, Andrea. Co-published simultaneously in *Journal of Religion & Abuse* (The Haworth Pastoral Press, an imprint of The Haworth Press, Inc.) Vol. 1, No. 2, 1999, pp. 31-52; and: *Remembering Conquest: Feminist/Womanist Perspectives on Religion, Colonization, and Sexual Violence* (ed: Nantawan Boonprasat Lewis and Marie M. Fortune) The Haworth Pastoral Press, an imprint of The Haworth Press, Inc., 1999, pp. 31-52. Single or multiple copies of this article are available for a fee from The Haworth Document Delivery Service [1-800-342-9678, 9:00 a.m. - 5:00 p.m. (EST). E-mail address: getinfo@haworthpressinc.com].

millions of dollars into tribally-based sexual and domestic violence programs. While domestic violence programs are proliferating, virtually no tribes have developed comprehensive sexual assault programs.

Native survivors of sexual violence often find no support when they seek healing and justice. When survivors seek help from non-Indian agencies, they are often told to disassociate themselves from their communities where their abusers are. The underlying philosophy of the white-dominated anti-rape movement is implicit in Susan Brownmiller's statement: [Rape] is nothing more or less than a conscious process of intimidation by which all men keep all women in a state of fear.[1] The notion that rape is "nothing more or less" than a tool of patriarchal control fails to consider how rape also serves as a tool of racism and colonialism. At the same time, when Native survivors of sexual violence seek healing within their communities, other community members accuse survivors of undermining sovereignty and being divisive by making public their abuse. According to the Mending the Hoop Technical Assistance Project in Minnesota, tribally-based sexual assault advocates believe that a major difficulty in developing comprehensive programs to address sexual assault in tribal communities, particularly sexual violence against adult women, is that many community members believe that sexual violence is "traditional." Historical evidence suggests, however, that sexual violence was rare in Native communities prior to colonization, and that it has served as a primary weapon in the U.S. war against Native nations ever since. Not only have tribal communities adopted European practices of sexual violence; they have largely lost sight of the fact that sexual violence is, in fact, not an Indian tradition. Both these responses reveal a lack of understanding of how sexual violence itself is an act of colonialism and genocide. Far from being traditional, sexual violence is an attack on Native sovereignty itself. As one elder stated at a conference I attended, "as long as we destroy ourselves from inside, we don't have to worry about anyone on the outside."

THE COLONIAL CONTEXT OF SEXUAL VIOLENCE

Ann Stoler argues that racism, far from being a reaction to crisis in which racial others are scapegoated for social ills, is a permanent part of the social fabric. "[R]acism is not an effect but a tactic in the internal fission of society into binary opposition, a means of creating 'biologized' internal enemies, against whom society must defend itself."[2] She notes that in the modern state, it is through the constant purification and elimination of racialized enemies within the state that ensures the growth of the national body. "Racism does not merely arise in moments of crisis, in sporadic cleansings. It is internal to the biopolitical state, woven into the web of the social body, threaded through its fabric."[3] Similarly, Kate Shanley notes that Native peoples are a permanent "present absence" in the U.S. colonial imagination, an "absence" that reinforces at every turn the conviction that Native peoples are indeed vanishing and that the conquest of native lands is justified.[4] Ella Shoat and Robert Stam describe this absence as "an ambivalently repressive mechanism [which] dispels the anxiety in the face of the Indian, whose very presence is a reminder of the initially precarious grounding of the American nation-state itself . . . In a temporal paradox, living Indians were induced to 'play dead,' as it were, in order to perform a narrative of manifest destiny in which their role, ultimately, was to disappear."[5] This "absence" is effected through the metaphorical transformation of Native bodies into a pollution which the colonial body must purify itself. As white Californians described in the 1860s, Native people were "the dirtiest lot of human beings on earth" (Rawls, 195). They wear "filthy rags, with their persons unwashed, hair uncombed and swarming with vermin."[6] The following 1885 Proctor & Gamble ad for Ivory Soap also illustrates this equation between Indian bodies and dirt.

> We were once factious, fierce and wild,
> In peaceful arts unreconciled
> Our blankets smeared with grease and stains
> From buffalo meat and settlers' veins.
> Through summer's dust and heat content
> From moon to moon unwashed we went,
> But IVORY SOAP came like a ray
> Of light across our darkened way
> And now we're civil, kind and good
> And keep the laws as people should,
> We wear our linen, lawn and lace
> As well as folks with paler face
> And now I take, where'er we go
> This cake of IVORY SOAP to show
> What civilized my squaw and me
> And made us clean and fair to see.[7]

In the colonial imagination, Native bodies are also immanently polluted with sexual sin. Albert Cave, Robert Warrior, H.C. Porter, and
others have demonstrated that Christian colonizers often likened Native peoples to the biblical Canaanites, both worthy of mass destruction.[8] What makes Canaanites supposedly worthy of destruction in the
biblical narrative and Indian peoples supposedly worthy of destruction
in the eyes of their colonizers is that they both personify sexual sin. In
the Bible, Canaanites commit acts of sexual perversion in Sodom (Gen
19:1-29), are the descendants of the unsavory relations between Lot
and his daughters (Gen 19:30-38), are the descendants of the sexually
perverse Ham (Gen 9:22-27), and prostitute themselves in service of
their gods (Gen 28:21-22; Deut 28:18; 1Kings 14:24; 2Kings 23:7;
Hosea 4:13; Amos 2:7).

Similarly, Native peoples, in the eyes of the colonizers, are marked
by their sexual perversity. Alexander Whitaker, a minister in Virginia
wrote in 1613: "They live naked in bodie, as if their shame of their
sinne deserved no covering: Their names are as naked as their bodie:
They esteem it a virtue to lie, deceive and steale as their master the
divell teacheth them."[9] Furthermore, according to Bernardino de Mi-
naya: "Their [the Indians] marriages are not a sacrament but a sacri-
lege. They are idolatrous, libidinous, and commit sodomy. Their chief
desire is to eat, drink, worship heathen idols, and commit bestial
obscenities."[10]

This understanding of Native peoples as dirty whose sexuality
threatens U.S. security was echoed in the comments of one doctor in
his attempt to rationalize the mass sterilization of Native women in the
1970s:

> People pollute, and too many people crowded too close together
> cause many of our social and economic problems. These in turn
> are aggravated by involuntary and irresponsible parenthood . . .
> We also have obligations to the society of which we are part. The
> welfare mess, as it has been called, cries out for solutions, one of
> which is fertility control."[11]

Herbert Aptheker describes the logical consequences of this sterilization movement:

> The ultimate logic of this is crematoria; people are themselves
> constituting the pollution and inferior people in particular, then
> crematoria become really vast sewerage projects. Only so may

one understand those who attend the ovens and concocted and conducted the entire enterprise; those "wasted"–to use U.S. army jargon reserved for colonial hostilities–are not really, not fully people.[12]

Because Indian bodies are "dirty," they are considered sexually violable and "rapable." That is, in patriarchal thinking, only a body that is "pure" can be violated. The rape of bodies that are considered inherently impure or dirty simply does not count. For instance, prostitutes have almost an impossible time being believed if they are raped because the dominant society considers the prostitute's body undeserving of integrity and violable at all times. Similarly, the history of mutilation of Indian bodies, both living and dead, makes it clear to Indian people that they are not entitled to bodily integrity. Andrew Jackson, for instance, ordered the mutilation of approximately 800 Muscogee Indian corpses, cutting off their noses and slicing long strips of flesh from their bodies to make bridle reins.[13] Tecumseh's skin was flayed and made into razor-straps.[14] A soldier cut off the testicles of White Antelope to make a tobacco pouch.[15] Col. John Chivington led an attack against the Cheyenne and Arapahoe in which nearly all the victims were scalped, their fingers, arms, and ears were amputated to obtain rings, necklaces and other jewelry, and their private parts were cut out to be exhibited before the public in Denver.[16] In the history of massacres against Indian people, colonizers attempt not only to defeat Indian people but to eradicate their very identity and humanity. They attempt to transform Indian people from human beings into tobacco pouches, bridle reins or souvenirs–an object for the consumption of white people.

As Stoler explains this process of racialized colonization,

> [T]he more 'degenerates' and 'abnormals' [in this case Native peoples] are eliminated, the lives of those who speak will be stronger, more vigorous, and improved. The enemies are not political adversaries, but those identified as external and internal threats to the population. Racism is the condition that makes it acceptable to put [certain people] to death in a society of normalization.[17]

She further notes that "the imperial discourses on sexuality cast white women as the bearers of more racist imperial order."[18] By extension,

Native women as bearers of a counter-imperial order pose a supreme threat to the imperial order. Symbolic and literal control over their bodies is important in the war against Native people, as these examples attest:

> When I was in the boat I captured a beautiful Carib woman . . . I conceived desire to take pleasure. . . . I took a rope and thrashed her well, for which she raised such unheard screams that you would not have believed your ears. Finally we came to an agreement in such a manner that I can tell you that she seemed to have been brought up in a school of harlots.[19]

> Two of the best looking of the squaws were lying in such a position, and from the appearance of the genital organs and of their wounds, there can be no doubt that they were first ravished and then shot dead. Nearly all of the dead were mutilated.[20]

> One woman, big with child, rushed into the church, clasping the alter and crying for mercy for herself and unborn babe. She was followed, and fell pierced with a dozen lances . . . the child was torn alive from the yet palpitating body of its mother, first plunged into the holy water to be baptized, and immediately its brains were dashed out against a wall.[21]

> The Christians attacked them with buffets and beatings . . . Then they behaved with such temerity and shamelessness that the most powerful ruler of the island had to see his own wife raped by a Christian officer.[22]

> I heard one man say that he had cut a woman's private parts out, and had them for exhibition on a stick. I heard another man say that he had cut the fingers off of an Indian, to get the rings off his hand. I also heard of numerous instances in which men had cut out the private parts of females, and stretched them over their saddle-bows and some of them over their hats.[23]

While the cra of Indian massacres in their more explicit form in North America is over, in Latin America, the wholesale rape and mutilation of indigenous women's bodies continues. During the 1982 massacre of Mayan people in the Aldea Rio Negro (Guatemala), 177 women and children were killed, the young women were raped in front of their mothers and the mothers were killed in front of their children. The younger children were then tied at the ankles and dashed against the rocks until their skulls were broken. This massacre was funded by the U.S. government.[24] While many white feminists are correctly outraged by the rapes in Bosnia, organizing to hold a war crimes tribunal against the Serbs, one wonders why the mass rapes in Guatemala, Chiapas or elsewhere against indigenous people in Latin America has not sparked the same outrage. In fact, feminist legal scholar Catherine MacKinnon argues that in Bosnia, "the world has *never* seen sex used this consciously, this cynically, this elaborately, this openly, this systematically . . . as a means of destroying a whole people."[25] She seems to forget that she only lives on this land because millions of Native people were raped, sexually mutilated and murdered. Is perhaps mass rape against European women genocide while mass rape against indigenous women is business as usual? In even the white feminist imagination, are native women's bodies more rapable than white women's bodies?

The colonization of Native women's bodies continues today. When I served as a non-violent witness for the Chippewa spearfishers in the 1980s who were being harassed by white racist mobs, one white harasser carried a sign saying "Save a fish; spear a pregnant squaw." During the 1990 Mohawk crisis in Oka, a white mob surrounded the ambulance of a Native woman who was attempting to leave the Mohawk reservation because she was hemorrhaging after having given birth. She was forced to "spread her legs" to prove she had given birth. The police at the scene refused to intervene. An Indian man was arrested for "wearing a disguise" (he was wearing jeans), and he was brutally beaten, with his testicles crushed. Two women from Chicago WARN (the organization I belong to) went to Oka to videotape the crisis. They were arrested and held in custody for eleven hours without being charged, and were told that they could not go to the bathroom unless the male police officers could watch. The place they were held was covered with pornographic magazines.

This colonial desire to subjugate Indian women's bodies was quite apparent when, in 1982, Stuart Kasten marketed a new video, "Custer's Revenge," in which players get points each time they, in the form of Custer, rape an Indian woman. The slogan of the game is "When you score, you score." He describes the game as "a fun sequence where the woman is enjoying a sexual act willingly." According to the promotional material:

You are General Custer. Your dander's up, your pistol's wavin'. You've hog-tied a ravishing Indian maiden and have a chance to rewrite history and even up an old score. Now, the Indian maiden's hands may be tied, but she's not about to take it lying down, by George! Help is on the way. If you're to get revenge you'll have to rise to the challenge, dodge a tribe of flying arrows and protect your flanks against some downright mean and prickly cactus. But if you can stand pat and last past the strings and arrows–You can stand last. Remember? Revenge is sweet.[26]

Ironically, while enslaving women's bodies, colonizers argued that they were actually somehow freeing Native women from the "oppression" they supposedly faced in Native nations. Thomas Jefferson argued that Native women "are submitted to unjust drudgery. This I believe is the case with every barbarous people. It is civilization alone which replaces women in the enjoyment of their equality."[27] The *Mariposa Gazette* similarly noted that when Indian women were safely under the control of white men, they "are neat, and tidy, and industrious, and soon learn to discharge domestic duties properly and creditably."[28] In 1862, a Native man in Conrow Valley was killed and scalped with his head twisted off, with his killers saying "You will not kill any more women and children."[29] Apparently, Native women can only be free while under the dominion of white men and both Native and white women have to be protected from Indian men, rather than from white men.

A 1985 Virginia Slims ad reflected a similar notion that white patriarchy saves Native women from oppression. On the left side of the ad was a totem pole of cartoonish figures of Indian women. Their names: Princess Wash and Scrub, Little Running Water Fetcher, Keeper of the Teepee, Princess Breakfast, Lunch and Dinner Preparer, Woman Who Gathers Firewood, Princess Buffalo Robe Sewer, Little Woman Who Weaves All Day; and Woman Who Plucks Feathers for Chief's Headdress. The caption on top of the totem pole reads: "Virginia Slims remembers one of many societies where the women stood head and shoulders above the men." On the right side of the hand, a model, dressed in make up, a tight skirt, nylons and high heels, with the familiar caption: "You've come a long way, baby." The message is that Native women, oppressed in their tribal societies, need to be liberated into the patriarchal standard of beauty where their true freedom lies. Ironically, however, while stereotypes prevail that Native women were beasts of burden for their men; in fact, prior to colonization, Indian societies for the most part were not male dominated. Women served as spiritual, political, and military leaders. Many societies were matrilineal and matrilocal. Although there existed a division of labor between women and men, women's and men's labor was accorded similar status.[30] Thus, the historical record would suggest, as Paula Gunn Allen argues, that the real roots of feminism should be found in Native societies. In this Virginia Slims ad, however, feminism is tied to colonial conquest–(white) women's liberation is founded upon the destruction of supposedly patriarchal Native societies.

Just as historically white colonizers who raped Indian women claimed that the real rapist was the Indian man, today white men who rape and murder Indian women often make this same claim. In Minneapolis, a white man, Jesse Coulter, raped, murdered and mutilated several Indian women. He claimed to be Indian, adopting the name Jesse Sittingcrow, and emblazoning an AIM tatoo on his arm.[31]

Similarly, Roy Martin, a full-blooded Native man, was charged with sexual assault. The survivor identified the rapist as white, about 25 years old, with a shag haircut. Martin, was 35 with hair past his shoulders.[32] Although the case was eventually dismissed, the fact that his case even made it to trial indicates the extent to which Native men are seen as the rapists of white women. Of course, Indian men do commit acts of sexual violence. After years of colonialism and boarding school experience, violence has also been internalized within Indian communities. However, this view of the Indian man as the "true" rapist serves to obscure who has the real power in this racist and patriarchal society. The U.S. is indeed engaged in a "permanent social war" against the Native bodies, particularly Native women's bodies, which threaten its legitimacy.[33] Colonizers evidently recognize the wisdom of the Cheyenne saying, "A Nation is not conquered until the hearts of the women [and their bodies as well] are on the ground."

Through this colonization and abuse of their bodies, Indian people learn to internalize self-hatred. Body image is integrally related to self-esteem. When one's body is not respected, one begins to hate oneself.[34] Anne, a Native boarding school student, reflects on this process:

> You better not touch yourself . . . If I looked at somebody . . . lust,
> sex, and I got scared of those sexual feelings. And I did not know
> how to handle them . . . What really confused me was if inter-
> course was sin, why are people born? . . . It took me a really long
> time to get over the fact that . . . I've sinned: I had a child.[35]

As her words indicate, when the bodies of Indian people are inherently
sinful and dirty, it becomes a sin just to be Indian. Thus, it is not a
surprise that Indian people who have survived sexual abuse often say
that they no longer wish to be Indian. The Menominee poet Chrytos
writes in such a voice in her poem "Old Indian Granny."

> You told me about all the Indian women you counsel
> who say they don't want to be Indian anymore
> because a white man or an Indian one raped them
> or killed their brother
> or somebody tried to run them over in the street
> or insulted them or all of it
> our daily bread of hate
> Sometimes I don't want to be an Indian either
> but I've never said so out loud before
> Since I'm so proud and political
> i have to deny it now
> Far more than being hungry
> having no place to live or dance
> no decent job no home to offer a Granny
> It's knowing with each invisible breath
> that if you don't make something pretty
> they can hang on their walls or wear around their necks
> you might as well be dead.[36]

The fact that many Native peoples will argue that sexual violence is
"traditional" indicates the extent to which our communities have
internalized self-hatred. As Frantz Fanon argues, "In the colonial
context, as we have already pointed out, the natives fight among
themselves. They tend to use each other as a screen, and each hides
from his neighbor the national enemy."[37] Then, as Michael Taussig
notes, Native peoples are portrayed by the dominant culture as inherently violent, self-destructive and dysfunctional. For example, Mike
Whelan made the following statement at a 1990 zoning hearing, call-

ing for the denial of a permit for an Indian battered women's shelter in South Dakota:

> Indian Culture as I view it, is presently so mongrelized as to be a mix of dependency on the Federal Government and a primitive society wholly on the outside of the mainstream of western civilization and thought. The Native American Culture as we know it now, not as it formerly existed, is a culture of hopelessness, godlessness, of joblessness, and lawlessness . . . Alcoholism, social disease, child abuse, and poverty are the hallmarks of this so called culture that you seek to promote, and I would suggest to you that the brave men of the ghost dance would hang their heads in shame at what you now pass off as that culture . . . I think that the Indian way of life as you call it, to me means cigarette burns in arms of children, double checking the locks on my cars, keeping a loaded shotgun by my door, and car bodies and beer cans on the front lawn . . . This is not a matter of race, it is a matter of keeping our community and neighborhood away from that evil that you and your ideas promote.[38]

Taussig comments on the irony of this logic: "Men are conquered not by invasion but by themselves. It is a strange sentiment, is it not, when faced with so much brutal evidence of invasion."[39] But as Fanon notes, this destructive behavior is not "the consequence of the organization of his [sic] nervous system or of characteral originality, but the direct product of the colonial system."[40]

Completing the destruction of a people involves the destruction of the integrity of their culture and spirituality which forms the matrix of Native women's resistance to sexual colonization. Native counselors generally agree that a strong cultural and spiritual identity is essential if Native people are to heal from abuse. This is because Native women's healing entails healing, not only from any personal abuse she has suffered, but also from the patterned history of abuse against her family, her nation, and the environment in which she lives.[41] Because Indian spiritual traditions are holistic, they have the ability to restore survivors of abuse to community, to restore their bodies to wholeness. That is why the most effect programs for healing revolve around reviving indigenous spiritual traditions.

In the colonial discourse, however, Native spiritual traditions become yet another site for the commodification of Indian women's bodies. As part of the genocidal process, Indian cultures become no longer the means of restoring wholeness, but become objects of consumerism for the dominant culture. Hanauni Kay Trask, Native Hawaiian activist, describes this process as "cultural prostitution."

> "Prostitution" in this context refers to the entire institution which defines a woman (and by extension the "female") as an object of degraded and victimized sexual value for use and exchange through the medium of money . . . My purpose is not to exact detail or fashion a model but to convey the utter degradation of our culture and our people under corporate tourism by employing "prostitution" as an analytical category . . .
>
> The point, of course, is that everything in Hawai'i can be yours, that is, you the tourist, the non-native, the visitor. The place, the people, the culture, even our identity as a "Native" people is for sale. Thus, Hawai'i, like a lovely woman, is there for the taking.[42]

Thus, this "New Age" appropriation of Indian spiritualities represents yet another form of sexual abuse for Indian women, hindering its ability to help women heal from abuse. Columnist Andy Rooney represents this dominant ideology when he argues that Native spiritual traditions "involving ritualistic dances with strong sexual overtones [are] demeaning to Indian women and degrading to Indian children."[43] Along similar lines, Mark and Dan Jury produced a film "Dances: Sacred and Profane" (August 1994) which advertised that it "climaxes with the first-ever filming of the Indian Sundance ceremony." This so called ceremony consisted of a white man, hanging from meat hooks from a tree, praying to the "Great White Spirit," and was then followed by C.C. Sadist, a group that performs sadomasochistic acts for entertainment.[44] Similarly, "plastic medicine" are often notorious for sexually abusing their clients in fake Indian ceremonies. Jeffrey Wall was recently sentenced for sexually abusing three girls while claiming this abuse was part of American Indian spiritual rituals that he was conducting as a supposed Indian medicine man.[45] David "Two Wolves" Smith and Alan Campnhey "Spotted Wolfe" were also charged for sexually abusing girls during supposed "cleansing" ceremonies.[46] That so many people do not question that sexual fondling would be part of Indian ceremonies to the point where legitimate spiritual leaders are forced to issue out statements such as "no ceremony requires anyone to be naked or fondled during the ceremony,"[47] signifies the extent to which the colonial discourse attempts to shift the meaning of Indian spirituality from something healing to something that is abusive.

Meanwhile, the colonizing religion of Native peoples, Christianity, which is supposed to "save" Native women from supposedly sexually exploitative traditional practices, has only made them more vulnerable to sexual violence. The large scale introduction of sexual violence in Native communities is largely a result of the Christian boarding school system, which had their beginnings in the 1600s under Jesuit priests along the St. Lawrence River. The system was more formalized in 1870 when Congress set aside funds to erect school facilities to be run by churches and missionary societies.[48] Attendance was mandatory, and children were forcibly taken from their homes for the majority of the year. They were forced to worship Christianity (native traditions were prohibited), and speak English only.[49] Children were subjected to constant physical and sexual abuse. Irene Mack Pyawasit, a former boarding school resident from the Menominee reservation testifies to her experience which is typical of many students' experiences:

> The government employees that they put into the schools had families but still there were an awful lot of Indian girls turning up pregnant. Because the employees were having a lot of fun, and they would force a girl into a situation, and the girl wouldn't always be believed. Then, because she came up pregnant, she would be sent home in disgrace. Some boy would be blamed for it, never the government employee. He was always scot-free. And no matter what the girl said, she was never believed.[50]

Even when teachers were charged with abuse, boarding schools refused to investigate. In the case of just one teacher, John Boone at the Hopi school, FBI investigations found that he had sexually abused over 142 children, but the principal of that school had not investigated any allegations of abuse.[51] Despite the epidemic of sexual abuse in boarding schools, the Bureau of Indian Affairs did not issue a policy on reporting sexual abuse until 1987, and did not issue a policy to strengthen the background checks of potential teachers until 1989.[52]

While not all Native people viewed their boarding school experiences as negative, it appears to be the case that, after the onset of boarding schools in Native communities, abuse becomes endemic within Indian families. Randy Fred, a former boarding school student, says that children in his school began to mimic the abuse they were experiencing.[53] After Father Harold McIntee from St Joseph's residential school on the Alkali Lake reserve was convicted of sexual abuse, two of his victims were later convicted of sexual abuse charges.[54]

ANTI-COLONIAL RESPONSES TO SEXUAL VIOLENCE

The struggle for sovereignty and the struggle against sexual violence cannot be separated. Conceptualizing sexual violence as a tool of genocide and colonialism then fundamentally alters the strategies for combating it. Currently, the rape crisis movement has promoted strengthening the criminal justice system as the primary means to end sexual violence. Rape crisis centers receive much state funding, and their strategies consequently tend to be state-friendly: hire more police, give longer sentences to rapists, etc. There is a contradiction, however, in relying upon the state to solve the problems it is responsible for creating. Native people per capita are the most arrested, most incarcerated, and most victimized by police brutality of any other ethnic group in the country.[55] Given the oppression Native people face within the criminal justice system, many communities are developing their own programs for addressing criminal behavior based on traditional modes of regulating their societies. However, as James and Elsie B. Zion note, Native domestic violence advocates are often reluctant to pursue traditional alternatives to incarceration for addressing violence against women.[56] Survivors of domestic and sexual violence programs are often pressured to "forgive and forget" in tribal mediation programs that focus more on maintaining family and tribal unity rather than on providing justice and safety for women. Rupert Ross's study of traditional approaches for addressing sexual/domestic violence on First Nations reserves in Canada notes these approaches are often very successful in addressing child sexual abuse where communities are less likely to blame the victim for the assault. In these cases, the community takes a pro-active effort in holding perpetrators accountable so that incarceration is often unnecessary. When a crime is reported, the working team that deals with sexual violence talks to the perpetrator and gives him the option of participating in the program. The perpetrator must first confess his guilt and then follow a

healing contract, or go to jail. The perpetrator can decline to participate completely in the program and go through normal routes in the
justice system. Everyone affected by the crime (victim, perpetrator,
family, friends, and the working team) is involved in developing the
healing contract. Everyone also holds the perpetrator accountable to
his contract. One Tlingit man noted that this approach was often more
difficult than going to jail:

> First one must deal with the shock and then the dismay on your
> neighbors faces. One must live with the daily humiliation, and at
> the same time seek forgiveness not just from victims, but from
> the community as a whole . . . [A prison sentence] removes the
> offender from the daily accountability, and may not do anything
> towards rehabilitation, and for many may actually be an easier
> disposition than staying in the community.[57]

Elizabeth Barker notes along similar lines that the problem with the
criminal justice system is that it diverts accountability from the community to players in the criminal justice system. Perpetrators are taken
away from their community and are further disabled from developing
ethical relationships within a community context.[58] Ross notes: "In
reality, rather than making the community a safer place, the threat of
jail places the community more at risk."[59]

Since the Hollow Lake reserve adopted this approach, 48 offenders
have been identified. Only five chose to go to jail, and only two who
entered the program have repeated crimes (one of the re-offenders
went through the program again and has not re-offended since). However, these approaches, notes Ross, often break down in cases where
the victim is an adult woman because community members are more
likely to blame her instead of the perpetrator for the assault.[60]

Many Native domestic violence advocates I have interviewed note
similar problems in applying traditional methods of justice to cases of
sexual assault and domestic violence. One advocate from a tribally-
based program in the Plains area contends that traditional approaches
are important for addressing violence against women, but they are
insufficient. To be effective, they must be backed up by the threat of
incarceration. She notes that medicine men have come to her program
saying, "we have worked with this offender and we have not been
successful in changing him. He needs to join your batterers' program." Traditional approaches toward justice presume that the com-

munity will hold a perpetrator accountable for his crime. However, in cases of violence against adult women, community members often do not regard this violence as a crime and will not hold the offender accountable. Before such approaches can be effective, we must implement community education programs that will sufficiently change community attitudes about these issues.

Another advocate from a reservation in the midwest argues that traditional alternatives to incarceration might in fact be more harsh than incarceration. Many Native people presume that traditional modes of justice focused on conflict resolution. In fact, she argues, penalties for societal infractions were not lenient–they entailed banishment, shaming, reparations, and sometimes death. This advocate was involved in an attempt to revise tribal codes by reincorporating traditional practices, but she found that it was difficult to determine what these practices were, and how they could be made useful today. For example, some practices, such as banishment, would not have the same impact as today. Prior to colonization, Native communities were so close-knit and interdependent that banishment was often the equivalent of a death sentence. Today, however, Native peoples can simply leave home and join the dominant society. In addition, the elders with whom she consulted admitted that their memories of traditional penal systems were tainted with the experience of being in boarding school.

Since incarceration today is understood as punishment, this advocate believes that it is the most appropriate way to address sexual violence. She argues that if a Native man rapes someone, he subscribes to white values rather than Native values because rape is not an Indian tradition. If he follows white values, then he should suffer the white way of punishment.

However, there are a number of difficulties in pursuing incarceration as the solution for addressing sexual assault. First, so few rapes are reported that the criminal justice system rarely has the opportunity to address the problem. Among tribal programs I have interviewed, an average of about 2 cases of rape are even reported each year. Complicating matters, because rape is a major crime, rape cases are generally handed to the States Attorney, who then declines the vast majority of cases. By the time tribal law enforcement programs even see rape cases, a year might have passed since the assault, making it difficult for these programs to prosecute. Also because rape is covered under the Major Crimes Act, many tribes have not even developed codes to address sexual assault as they have for domestic violence. One advocate who conducted a training for southwestern tribes on sexual assault says that the participants said they did not need to develop codes because the "feds will take care of rape cases." She then asked how many cases of rape have been federally prosecuted, and the participants discovered that not one case of rape had ever reached the federal courts. In addition, there is inadequate jail space in many tribal communities. When the tribal jail is full, the tribe has to pay the surrounding county to house its prisoners. Given the financial constraints, tribes are reluctant to house prisoners for any length of time.

But perhaps most importantly, as sociologist Luana Ross (Salish) notes, incarceration has been largely ineffective in reducing crime rates in the dominant society, much less Native communities. "The white criminal justice system does not work for white people; what makes us think it's going go work for us?" she asks.

> The criminal justice system in the United States needs a new approach. Of all the countries in the world, we are the leader in incarceration rates–higher than South Africa and the former Soviet Union, countries that are perceived as oppressive to their own citizens. Euro-America builds bigger and better prisons and fills them up with criminals. Society would profit if the criminal justice system employed restorative justice . . . Most prisons in the United States are, by design, what a former prisoner termed "the devil's house." Social environments of this sort can only produce dehumanizing conditions.[61]

As a number of studies have demonstrated, more prisons and more police do not lead to lower crime rates.[62] For instance, the Rand Corporation found that California's three strikes legislation, which requires life sentences for three-time convicted felons, did not reduce the rate of "murders, rapes, and robberies that many people believe to be the law's principal targets."[63] In fact, changes in crime rate often have more to do with fluctuations in employment rates than with increased police surveillance or increased incarceration rates.[64] Concludes Steven Walker, "Because no clear link exists between incarceration and crime rates, and because gross incapacitation locks up many low-rate offenders at a great dollar cost to society, we conclude as follows: gross incapacitation is not an effective policy for reducing serious crime."[65] Criminologist Elliott Currie similarly finds that "the *best* face put on the impact of massive prison increases, in a study routinely used by prison supporters to prove that 'prison works,' shows that prison growth seems not to have 'worked' at all for homicide or assault, barely if at all for rape . . . "[66] The premise of the justice system is that most people are law-abiding except for "deviants" who do not follow the law. However, given the epidemic rates of sexual and domestic violence in which 50 percent of women will be battered and 47 percent will be raped in their lifetime, it is clear that most men are implicated in our rape culture. It is not likely that we can send all of these men to jail. As Fay Koop argues, addressing rape through the justice system simply furthers the myth that rape/domestic violence is caused by a few bad men rather than acts which most men find themselves implicated in.[67] Thus, relying upon the criminal justice system to end violence against women may strengthen the colonial apparatus in tribal communities that furthers violence while providing nothing more than the illusion of safety to survivors of sexual and domestic violence. As the London based Women Against Rape states:

> The prison sentences imposed for rape and sexual assault are often very low relative to sentencing for other offences. It is plain that these very low sentences can endanger women, and also tell potential rapists that rape and sexual assault are not serious crimes in the eyes of the Law. It is equally clear that longer prison sentences are no solution to the tragic problems women have with the courts and the police, and no solution to the causes of rape. An increase in punishment does not satisfy demands for women's safety. A generalised call for heavier sentencing has traditionally been the way in which politicians have appeared to be doing something about rape, without spending any money on rape prevention, or showing any genuine interest in the protection of women. In fact long sentences are often advocated for reasons which have nothing to do with women's safety.[68]

Sexual violence is a fundamental attack on Indian sovereignty, and both Native and non-Native communities are challenged to develop programs that address sexual violence from an anti-colonial, anti-racist framework so that we don't attempt to eradicate acts of personal violence by strengthening the apparatus of state violence. Nothing less than a holistic approach towards eradicating sexual violence can be successful. As Ines Hernandez-Avila states:

We must imagine a world without rape. But I cannot imagine a world without rape, a world without misogyny, without imagining a world without racism, classism, sexism, homophobia, ageism, historical amnesia and other forms and manifestations of violence directed against those communities that are seen to be "asking for it." Even the Earth is presumably "asking for it". . .

What do I imagine then? From my own Native American perspective, I see a world where sovereign indigenous peoples continue to plunge our memories to come back to our originality, to live in dignity and carry on our resuscitated and ever-transforming cultures and traditions with liberty . . . I see a world were native women find strength and continuance in the remembrance of who we really were and are . . . a world where more and more native men find the courage to recognize and honor–that they and the women of their families and communities have the capacity to be profoundly vital and creative human beings.[69]

NOTES

1. Susan Brownmiller. *Against Our Will*. Toronto: Bantam Books, 1986: 5.

2. Ann Stoler. *Race and the Education of Desire*. Chapel Hill: Duke University Press, 1997: 59.

3. Ibid: 59.

4. Lecture, Indigenous Intellectual Sovereignties Conference. UC Davis, April, 1998.

5. Ella Shoat and Robert Stam. *Unthinking Eurocentrism*. London: Routledge, 1994: 119-118.

6. James Rawls. *Indians of California: The Changing Image*. Norman: University of Oklahoma Press, 1997: 195.

7. Andre Lopez. *Pagans in Our Midst*. Mohawk Nation: Awkwesasne Notes: 119.

8. See Robert Allen Warrior, "Canaanites, Cowboys, and Indians," *Anthology of HONOR*, pp. 21-26, formerly in *Christianity and Crisis*, September 11, 1989. Albert Cave, "Canaanites in a Promised Land," *American Indian Quarterly*, Fall 1988, pp. 277-297; Porter, op. cit., pp. 91-115; Ronald Sanders, *Lost Tribes and Promised Lands*, Boston: Little, Brown and Company, 1978: 46, 181 and 292; Djelal Kadir, *Columbus and the Ends of the Earth*, Berkeley: University of California Press, 1992: 129.

9. Robert Berkhofer. *The White Man's Indian*. New York: Vintage, 1978: 19.

10. Stannard, 211.

11. "Oklahoma: Sterilization of Native Women Charged to I.H.S." *Akwesasne Notes.* Mid Winter 1989: 30.

12. Herbert Aptheker. *Racism, Imperialism and Peace.* Minneapolis, MEP Publications: 144.

13. David Stannard. *American Holocaust.* Oxford: Oxford University Press, 1992: 121.

14. William James. *A Full and Correct Account of the Military Occurrences of the Late War between Great Britain and the United States of America* (2 vols., London: printed by the author, 1818) vol 1: 293-296, quoted in David Wrone and Russel Nelson (eds). *Who's the Savage?* Malabar: Robert Krieger Publishing, 1982: 82.

15. US Congress. Senate, Special Committee Appointed under Joint Resolution of March 3, 1865. *Condition of the Indian Tribes,* S. Rept. 156, 39th Cong., 2d sess., 1867: 95-96; quoted in *Who's The Savage?* 113.

16. John Terrell. *Land Grab.* New York: Dial Press, 1972: 13.

17. Stoler, 85.

18. Stoler, 35.

19. From Cueneo, an Italian nobleman, quoted in Sale, p. 140.

20. US Commissioner of Indian Affairs, *Annual Report for 1871*, Washington: Government Printing Office, 1871, pp. 487-488, cited in *Who's the Savage?* p, 123.

21. LeRoy R. Haven, ed. *Ruxton of the Rockies.* Norman: University of Oklahoma Press, 1950, pp. 46-149 cited in *Who's the Savage,* p. 97.

22. Las Casas, p. 33.

23. Lieutenant James D. Cannon quoted in "Report of the Secretary of War," 39th Congress, Second Session, Senate Executive Document 26, Washington DC 1867 printed in *The Sand Creek Massacre: A Documentary History*, New York: Sol Lewis, 1973, pp. 129-130.

24. Dona Antonia, lecture U.C. Davis, 1996.

25. Catherine MacKinnon, "Turning Rape into Pornography: Postmodern Genocide," *Ms Magazine* 4 No. 1: 27 (emphasis mine).

26. Promotional material from Public Relations: Mahoney/Wasserman & Associates, Los Angeles, CA, n.d.

27. Quoted in Roy Harvey Pearce, *Savagism and Civilization.* Baltimore: Johns Hopkins Press, 1965: 93.

28. In Robert Heizer (ed), *The Destruction of California Indians.* Lincoln: University of Nebraska Press, 1993: 284.

29. Quoted in James Rawls. *Indians of California: The Changing Image.* Norman: University of Oklahoma Press, 1997: 182.

30. See Annette Jaimes and Theresa Halsey, "American Indian Women: At the Center of Indigenous Resistance in North America," in Annette Jaimes, ed., *State of Native America*, Boston: South End Press, 1992, p. 311-344, and Paula Gunn Allen, *The Sacred Hoop*, Boston: Beacon Press, 1986.

31. Mark Brunswick and Paul Klauda, "Possible suspect in serial killings jailed in N. Mexico," *Minneapolis Star and Tribune* May 28, 1987: 1A.

32. "Indian Man Being Tried for Rape with No Evidence," *Fargo Forum.* January 9, 1995.

33. Stoler, 69.

34. For further discussion on relationship between bodily abuse and self-esteem, see *Courage to Heal*, op. cit., esp. pp. 207-222 and Bonnie Burstow, *Radical Feminist Therapy*, London: Sage, 1992, esp. pp. 187-234.

35. Quoted in Haig-Brown, p. 108.

36. Chrystos. *Fugitive Colors*. Vancouver: Press Gang, 1995: 41.

37. Frantz Fanon. *Wretched of the Earth*. New York: Grove Press, 1963: 309.

38. "Discrimination and the Double Whammy." Lake Andes, South Dakota: Native American Women's Health and Education Resource Center, 1990: 2-3.

39. Michael Taussig. *Shamanism, Colonialism and the Wild Man*. Chicago: University of Chicago Press: 20.

40. Fanon, 309.

41. Justine Smith (Cherokee), personal conversation, February 17, 1994.

42. Haunani-Kay Trask. *From a Native Daughter: Colonialism & Sovereignty in Hawai'i*, (Maine: Common Courage Press, 1993), pp. 185-194.

43. Andy Rooney, "Indians Have Worse Problems," *Chicago Tribune*, March 4, 1992.

44. Jim Lockhart, "AIM Protests Film's Spiritual Misrepresentation," *News from Indian Country*, Late September 1994: 10.

45. "Shaman sentenced for sex abuse," *News from Indian Country*, Mid-June 1996: 2-A.

46. David Melmer, "Sexual Assualt," *Indian Country Today* 15 (April 30-May 7, 1996): 1.

47. Michael Pace in ibid.

48. Jorge Noriega, "American Indian Education in the United States: Indoctrination for Subordination to Colonialism," *State of Native America*, p. 380.

49. U.S. Bureau of Indian Affairs, "Rules for Indian Schools," *Annual Report of the Commissioner of Indian Affairs*, 1890, Washington DC, cxlvi, cl-clii, cited in Frederick Binder and David M. Reimers, eds., *The Way We Lived*, Lexington: D.C. Heath and Company, 1982, p. 59.

50. Fran Leeper Buss, comp., *Dignity: Lower Income Women Tell of Their Lives and Struggles*, Ann Arbor: University of Michigan Press, 1985, p. 156. For further accounts of the widespread nature of sexual and other abuse in boarding schools, see Native Horizons Treatment Centre, *Sexual Abuse Handbook*, Hagersville Ontario, pp. 61-68; "The End of The Silence," *Maclean's* 105, No. 37, September 14, 1992, pp.14 & 16; Jim DeNomie, "American Indian Boarding Schools: Elders Remember" *Aging News*, Winter 1990-91, p. 2-6; U.S. Congress, Senate, Committee on Indian Affairs, *Survey of the Conditions of the Indians in the United States, Hearings*, before a Subcommittee of the Committee on Indian Affairs, Senate, on SR 79, 70th Cong., 2d session, 1929, pp. 428-429, 1021-1023, and 2833-2835 cited in David Wrone and Russell Nelson, eds, *Who's the Savage*, Malabar: Robert Krieger Publishing, 1982, pp. 152-154.

51. "Goodbye BIA, Hello New Federalism," *American Eagle* Vol. 2 No. 6, December 1994, p. 19. Incidentally, after the allegations of abuse became public, the BIA merely provided a counselor for the abused children, who then used his sessions with them to write a book.

52. "Child Sexual Abuse in Federal Schools," *The Ojibwe News*, January 17, 1990, p. 8.

53. In Celia Haig-Brown, *Resistance and Renewal*, Vancouver: Tilacum, 1988, pp. 14-15.

54. The Province, July 19, 1989 and Vancouver Sun, March 17, 1990 quoted in *Sexual Abuse Handbook*, p. 66.

55. Troy Armstrong; Michael Guilfoyle and Ada Pecos Melton. "Native American Delinquency: An Overview of Prevalence, Causes, and Correlates," in Marianne O. Nielsen and Robert A. Silverman (eds) *Native Americans, Crime, and Justice*. Boulder: Westview Press, 1996: 81.

56. James Zion and Elsie Zion. "Hazho's Sokee'–Stay Together Nicely: Domestic Violence Under Navajo Common Law," in Marianne O. Nielsen and Robert A. Silverman (eds) *Native Americans, Crime, and Justice*. Boulder: Westview Press, 1996: 106.

57. Rupert Ross. *Return to the Teachings*. London: Penguin, 1997: 18.

58. Elizabeth Barker, "The Paradox of Punishment in Light of the Anticipatory Role of Abolitionism," in Herman Bianchi and Rene van Swaaningern (eds) *Abolitionism*. Amsterdam: Free University Press, 1986: 91.

59. Ross, *Return*, 38.

60. Ross, Rupert. "Leaving Our White Eyes Behind: The Sentencing of Native Accused," in Marianne O. Nielsen and Robert A. Silverman (eds) *Native Americans, Crime, and Justice*. Boulder: Westview Press, 1996: 168.

61. Ross, Luana. *Inventing the Savage: The Social Construction of Native American Criminality*. Austin: University of Texas Press, 1998: 268.

62. Steven Donziger. *The Real War on Crime*. New York: HarperCollins, 1996: 42 and 162; Samuel Walker. *Sense and Nonsense about Crime and Drugs*. Belmont, CA: Wadsworth Publishing Company, 1998; Elliott Currie. *Crime and Punishment in America*. New York: Metropolitan Books, 1998.

63. Quoted in Walker, 139.

64. Steve Box and Chris Hale. "Economic Crisis and the Rising Prisoner Population in England and Wales," *Crime and Social Justice* 17 (1982): 20-35. Mark Colvin. "Controlling the Surplus Population: the Latent Functions of Imprisonment and Welfare in Late U.S. Capitalism," in B.D. MacLean (ed.) *The Political Economy of Crime*. Scarborough: Prentice-Hall Canada, 1986. Ivan Jankovic. "Labour Market and Imprisonment," *Crime and Social Justice* 8 (1977): 17-31.

65. Walker, 130.

66. Currie, 59.

67. Fay Honey Koop, "On Radical Feminism and Abolition," *We Who Would Take No Prisoners: Selections from the Fifth International Conference on Penal Abolition*. Vancouver: Collective Press, 1993: 592.

68. Quoted in Tony Ward, "Symbols and Noble Lies: Abolitionism, 'Just Deserts' and Crimes of the Powerful," in *Abolitionism* op. cit.: 80.

69. Ines Hernandez-Avila. "In Praise of Insubordination, or What Makes a Good Woman Go Bad?" in Emilie Buchwald, Pamela R. Fletcher, and Martha Roth (eds). *Transforming a Rape Culture*. Minneapolis: Milkweed, 1993: 388-389.

Scars *ARE* History:
Colonialism, Written on the Body

On the occasion of the centennial of Philippine "independence"

Rachel Bundang

SUMMARY. Written as a reflection on the observation of the 1898-1998 centennial of the Philippines' independence from Spain and subsequent U.S. occupation, this essay presents a Filipina-American immigrant's perspective on the intersection of religion, colonization, and sexual violence in the making of the modern Philippine society. The author offers a critical look at the development of Filipina womanhood by examining the *babaylan*, Maria Clara, Miss Saigon, and Flor Contemplación as icons through which to view the Philippines' colonial history under Spain and continuing neo-colonial relations with the United States. *[Article copies available for a fee from The Haworth Document Delivery Service: 1-800-342-9678. E-mail address: getinfo@haworthpressinc.com <Website: http://www.haworthpressinc.com>]*

KEYWORDS. *Babaylan,* Colonialism–Philippines–Spain, Colonialism–Philippines–United States of America, Contemplación, Flor, Filipina, Maria Clara, *Miss Saigon,* Philippines–History–Women, Philippines–History–1521-1898, Philippines–History–1898-1946, Philippines–History–1946- , Philippines–Roman Catholicism

When I was invited to join this panel last spring, I agreed to do so because I was highly conscious of being one of the very few Filipina voices in the United States pursuing religious studies at an advanced

---

[Haworth co-indexing entry note]: "Scars *ARE* History: Colonialism, Written on the Body." Bundang, Rachel. Co-published simultaneously in *Journal of Religion & Abuse* (The Haworth Pastoral Press, an imprint of The Haworth Press, Inc.) Vol. 1, No. 2, 1999, pp. 53-69; and: *Remembering Conquest: Feminist/ Womanist Perspectives on Religion, Colonization, and Sexual Violence* (ed: Nantawan Boonprasat Lewis and Marie M. Fortune) The Haworth Pastoral Press, an imprint of The Haworth Press, Inc., 1999, pp. 53-69. Single or multiple copies of this article are available for a fee from The Haworth Document Delivery Service [1-800-342-9678, 9:00 a.m. - 5:00 p.m. (EST). E-mail address: getinfo@haworthpressinc.com].

level. I am an ethicist who takes the daily challenges of faith, family, and history as seriously as the rest of my academic formation; and I very much wanted this opportunity to reflect publicly on what the observation of this centennial has meant for me, being in this field at this time and doing this work.

I am undoubtedly a product of the religion, colonization, and sexual violence that I have come to revisit here with you today. I have not personally witnessed these horrors. But in a very real and immediate way, it is why and how so many members of my family have emigrated here–why and how there is such a thing as Philippine diaspora everywhere. As Dean Alegado notes,

> . . . the exodus of Filipinos to the United States . . . has not been an accidental phenomenon. It has not resulted purely from the decision of individual Filipino immigrants to leave their poverty-stricken country for "greener pastures" . . . Filipino immigration to the U.S. is a result of the unequal relations between a neo-colony and an imperial power. It is both an outcome and agent of unequal development.[1]

And as a bicultural, bilingual child of the 1.5-generation,[2] I am conflicted about my own presence and participation in the midst of this narrative of domination, subjugation, and resistance–conflicted about being asked to represent thousands of stories of pain that are mine yet not mine. For better *and* worse, those are the forces and historical movements that have forged a nation, however troubled, however dysfunctional, however loosely bound together. Oppression in a colonial key does not leave much room for one to act with integrity, and perhaps the most I can offer the discussion is a more culturally specific, culturally sensitive insight. At the risk of being very basic and reductionist, I shall use this brief opportunity as a teaching moment and bring to light the forgotten and co-opted history of a still-colonized people who gave birth to me. This is a chance to offer a primer on Filipina history, to do some critical reflection and rewriting on the nature of faith, memory, and womanhood at the juncture between the cultures of the Philippines and those of the Western nations who have made of us a laboratory for the sake of empires both ecclesiastical and political/economic.

Filipino nationalists often make the running joke that the Philippines spent nearly four hundred years in the convent (under Spanish-i.e., Roman Catholic–rule, 1521-1898), followed by fifty years in Hollywood (under the U.S., 1898-1946).[3] I would add that, given the kinds of economic, political, and military "agreements" that the Philippines has entered into with the U.S., we are still driving around the slums of Beverly Hills, stopping occasionally to gawk at all the conspicuous consumption on Rodeo Drive and press our noses to the window. Contrary to U.S. civic memory, this centennial is not really about the conquest of a Spanish empire on its deathbed. It is about the metastasis of "a social cancer."[4] It is about the *continuing* exercise of empire by a growing young nation feeling its oats, coupled with the further deprivation of sovereignty to a small, also young country. It is about a people, a political body wracked, even crippled, by post-traumatic stress disorder wrought by a textbook case of colonization. It is about perhaps the world's longest ongoing revolution and the history of popular resistance against imperialism. And here we resurrect the underside of the history taught in U.S. schools. In this "neocolonial formation" that is the Philippines, "feminist issues intersect with questions of national sovereignty at every single juncture."[5] The simplest way for me to illustrate the social and psychic costs of this cancer is to write the body of this essay in the form of alternative dictionary or encyclopedia entries. More specifically, I shall trace the trajectory of Filipina womanhood by summoning figures drawn from parts of our collective memory–our popular mythologies, our local histories, our imagination: *Mga babaylan. Maria Clara. Miss Saigon. Flor Contemplación.*

BABAYLAN *(TAGALOG, "PRIESTESS")*[6]

Even prior to contact with Spain, the Malays who inhabited the Philippines had already been influenced by the Chinese (some of whom came to settle as a merchant class) and the Muslims of the surrounding islands (some of whom established a stronghold in the Sulus that exists today). Research on pre-colonial cultures among the various Malay tribes of the archipelago reveals that they were not matriarchal but rather did operate on a quite egalitarian model. From childhood onward, women and men enjoyed equal status and received equal education and training. Any difference in treatment–and inheritance–depended not on gender but rather on birth order and legitimacy. While marriages were arranged, wives kept their names and "were treated as companions, not as slaves."[7] Women were acknowledged as key to the family's economic stability, and they also had great say in both domestic and external affairs. They exercised equal rights with regard to property, marriage and divorce, and making or holding pacts as well.

Women's political leadership in this early period is more the stuff of legend, not exactly verified or verifiable. But of these "legends," Princess Urduja of Pangasinan best represents the power held and latitude accorded tribal women. She was our own Xena or Amazon, renowned and respected for her courage as a warrior and her wisdom as a ruler.

On the religious front, the Tagalogs did not worship goddesses, but they did understand God, *Bathala,* as the union of male and female spirit.[8] And in terms of cult, women held court as religious leaders and healers. There were no priests; only a priestess or *babaylan,* also known as a *catalonan,* could offer sacrifices.

Spain arrived in 1521 and had established colonial rule by 1565. And conversion to Christianity–by this time so steeped in patriarchal tradition, thought, and practice–was a large part of its program for dominating and controlling property, including both the people and the land. At this point of first contact, probably no two cultures could have been more opposite. As the next section will explain more fully, "The new religion, Catholicism, was so violative of women's rights"–of cult, of property and domain, of bodily integrity and more–"that the priestesses led rebellions and resistance against Spain" almost from the very beginning. But in and for their acts of personal and collective self-defense, they and their followers were systematically massacred for the next two hundred years. By the end of the 17th century, their numbers had been so reduced that the survivors literally fled into the hills. "The great *babaylan* center in Mount Banahaw survived, although the old religion has been overlain by Christian mysticism."[9] (Indeed, some photographs of their religious practices have been circulated in recent years, and they reveal many trappings of Roman Catholicism: the wearing of albs and mitres, the use of monstrances and croziers, etc.) To their credit, the Muslims in and around Mindanao fended off Spanish incursions; and their resistance to outside control–by resettlement, conversion, or otherwise–continues today, even against the present government. Thus did the sorry history of colonial occupation begin. And thus did the Philippines become the only predominantly Christian nation in all of Asia.

SEE ALSO: *ecclesiastical patriarchalization; indigenous peoples' movements; "the prime directive."*

MARIA CLARA

The history of the Philippines in many ways parallels that of the Americas because Spain's conquests of both territories were contemporaneous. There are also records of contact through the Manila galleon trade between the islands and the New World.[10] But while the plans for and intent in conquest were quite similar, the actual execution and effects were quite different.

> In considerable contrast to conditions in the New World, the relatively small number of Spaniards in the Philippines ruled out large-scale miscegenation and the early emergence of a politically contentious mestizo class, along with the eventual marginalization of the local languages in favor of Castilian. It also precluded the drastic economic and ecological changes that accompanied the establishment of mining industries and enormous landed estates in the Americas. The Philippines thus escaped the demographic disasters stemming from the spread of new diseases, severe working conditions, and wars which befell the Amerindians in the sixteenth century. Finally, the relative paucity of Spanish settlers in the archipelago prevented the colonizers from relying on sheer coercion and required them to depend on evangelization to establish and validate their power. Thus the Spanish priest came to occupy a role of considerable importance in the spread and consolidation of colonial rule. For the vast majority of the native throughout most of the three centuries of Spanish rule, the Spanish cleric (natives were not ordained into the priesthood in any significant numbers until the late eighteenth century) came to represent their most tangible link to the Spanish *imperio.* But . . . if the Catholic church was to take root among the heathen, its message had to be rendered in terms that were familiar and minimally comprehensible to them. The result was the standard missionary practice of preaching the Gospel in the native tongues of the subject peoples.[11]

In short, Spain conquered the *Indios* of the Philippines[12] more by the cross than the sword. The Church was not only a tool or medium of conquest; it was a direct and active agent. It is with some irony, then, that the Philippines touts being the only Christian nation in Asia; depending on the source, statistics say that the population is 85-92% Catholic.

The Spanish period in the Philippines was nothing short of a friarocracy. Imported clerics of all orders–primarily Augustinians, Dominicans, Franciscans, and Jesuits–then sought to fashion the local world in the image and likeness of that which they left behind. Imitating their ideal of "a totalitarian economy of divine mercy," they controlled bodies by controlling the spaces in which they lived, resettling whole communities into more governable units, centralizing land ownership in their hands, and fashioning a hierarchy of persons and communities that got reflected in geography. One legacy this has left is the desperate need for agrarian reform. The feudal concentration of properties among the select and wealthy few demands redistribution. Returning real, not just nominal, control of the land to the people is a necessary step in ensuring the most basic level of economic autonomy to the rural poor, and, in turn, stability to their families, thus bettering the health and welfare of the poor–especially the women and children.

As they controlled bodies and space, the friars likewise controlled minds (and souls) by controlling language, so that Tagalog or any native tongue was derivative compared to Latin and Spanish.[13] With special schools and manuals, they modeled Filipina girls after "the Spanish women of the Iberian society of their time, where their lifestyle did not differ much from that of a contemplative nun today . . . The cult of the Blessed Virgin Mary was introduced to complete their domestication."[14] And, of course, trysts, intermarriages, and random miscegenations also took place. Rebel women–like Gabriela Silang of the 18th century, who led the longest sustained native revolt against Spain after the brutal capture and death of her husband–were hanged as heretics and witches–as enemies of the state, and therefore the Church.

Maria Clara is the heroine of *Noli Me Tangere*, José Rizál's meditation on the dysfunctions of colonialism. Since her introduction to the popular culture in 1886 when the novel was published, she has come to be read as the representation of the ideal Filipina as conceived by the clerical mind: "sweet, shy, docile, and pious,"[15] Iberianized, faithful and devoted to Mary (fondly called *Ina,* or "mother")–a pure, virginal, and chaste *mestiza* beauty. But by the same token, she is an icon of the people and nation as victim. As the bastard child of the town's former parish priest, she is the Filipina equivalent of the tragic mulatto. She sacrifices her chance at happiness in marriage by becoming a nun rather than letting dishonor come to those she loves because of her illegitimacy–a circumstance that is not her fault but rather a pure accident of birth. And in retreating from the world, she goes mad and ultimately commits suicide. Her value as a woman is compromised by nothing of her own doing, but simply by her own being.

The effects of the friars' sexual abuses and improprieties are still felt today. A Filipina-American colleague of mine in another field recently met for the first time whole branches of her family she had never known to exist. In comparing notes with them, she discovered that their common ancestor was a 19th-century Spanish friar who had kept multiple mistresses concurrently.

The tragedy of Maria Clara in her self-loathing and the power she holds in the popular imagination as an icon show how Filipinos have been seduced and jilted in the colonial encounter. This is still the case. We have learned the insidious language, the destructive dance of domination and subjugation all too well; authoritarianism has spawned absolute dependence upon external, constituted authority for decision-making. Mary John Mananzan finds that

> apart from the individual women who have defied their domestication and in spite of the growth of the women's movement even among church women, the great majority have internalized the stereotyped roles Church and society have assigned them.[16]

In the Filipinization of faith, other icons and narratives of suffering and penitence in our culture–both in the Philippines and here in our immigrant communities–only further attest to the colonizations of soul and spirit along with those of lands and bodies. A good icon, it seems, is a dead icon. In this context, narratives of resistance through survival, as opposed to narratives of triumph through memory in martyrdom and victimhood, may tell a good story; but the former are ultimately heard as heretical and iconoclastic, for they fundamentally reject any interpretation of temporal suffering and death as redemptive.

SEE ALSO: *beauty pageants and fiestas* (Flores de Mayo, Santacruzan, etc.); *Blessed Virgin Mary;* mestizaje; penitentes at pasyon.

"MISS SAIGON"

This musical has proven problematic in contemporary A/PI (Asian/ Pacific Islander) communities–especially among our artists–for a variety of reasons, namely that of equal opportunity for employment in the arts. But what I shall treat here is what Kim, the title character, represents. The story reworks Giacomo Puccini's *Madame Butterfly* plot, setting it instead in Vietnam. Chris, an American marine, has a one-night arrangement with Kim, a Vietnamese bar-girl in Saigon shortly before the fall of the city and the emergency withdrawal of the American troops from it. Kim has come to the city after her village was destroyed and her whole family killed in the war. She fantasizes of finding a strong GI to protect her. The two quickly fall in love and even celebrate a sort of mock wedding. In the next scene, we see Kim left behind in Ho Chi Minh City with their son Tam, while Chris has gone home, gotten married to Ellen, and continued with his life. Kim tries to arrange for an escape and reunion with him, rejecting her original arranged marriage in the process. Fleeing with Tam, she lands in Bangkok and gets a job in a massage parlor. Meanwhile, Chris and Ellen go there to redeem her son. When Kim realizes that Chris has truly married and does not mean to take her back, she kills herself and leaves them the boy to care for.

Filipina singer-actress Lea Salonga was cast as the first Kim ever. Following up on her success and enduring popularity, the producers now regularly hold casting calls in Manila and other places with a sizable Asian female population. The upshot: Kim has been played most often–if not always–by Filipinas, whether on tour or at home on Broadway. The message between the lines is that all these women in this kind of situation are usable bodies, interchangeable parts, messy complications behind the male games of military history and foreign affairs. Kim is an icon, albeit glamorized, in a soap/operatic way, of the sex tour industry that has grown up around military installations in the Philippines and in other Asian nations with a history of significant U.S. military presence. That trade still thrives today, even though Subic Naval Base and Clark Air Field were shut down in 1992.

In the few years since then, the U.S. Navy has decided that it is worth it to them to rehabilitate the two bases after Mount Pinatubo practically buried them in a series of eruptions. Some saw this as an act of God returning the land to the people. Nonetheless, many have argued too that the economic developments that have replaced military work are just as bad; for while the flesh trade has diminished or simply been displaced to other towns and neighborhoods, the consumer culture has moved in as "light industry" with a vengeance, providing myriad tired options for consumption of cheap goods to gorge on itself.

At this writing, the GABRIELA Network reveals that the Philippine and U.S. Governments are negotiating a Visiting Forces Agreement (VFA)/Status of Forces Agreement (SoFA). Despite prohibitions laid out in the Philippine Constitution, this agreement would open 22 Philippine ports to military exercises and allow an indefinite number of U.S. military troops to visit or temporarily stay in the Philippines– and all this a mere six years after the closure of the U.S. bases. E. San Juan writes that the two military installations represent "colonial suzerainty," and "as a springboard for intervention in the China market and the Asian-Pacific geopolitical theater" are "the main reason for U.S. annexation of the islands."[17] But in negotiating the VFA, the U.S. is clearly unwilling to lose its grip in the region. Part of their argument in wanting to return is that they need an Asian outpost from which to fight threats against allegedly unsavory characters like Osama Ben Laden. In the wake of these developments, GABRIELA activists and others struggling against the retrenchment of imperialism are mobilizing a "JUNK VFA!" campaign to rally support in both the U.S. and the Philippines against the return of militarization, prostitution, and violence against women.[18]

Examples of aggressive American interventions and machinations go back much further, though. On May 1, 1898, Admiral George Dewey defeated the Spanish fleet in Manila Bay. But at the time of the U.S. invasion, the Philippines was already in the midst of its own revolution against Spain. Dewey offered his assistance to the Philippine Revolutionary Army (PRA), led by General Emilio Aguinaldo, and brought President McKinley's word that the U.S. had "no design of aggrandizement and no ambition of conquest." With this alliance, the PRA succeeded in thoroughly defeating Spanish forces throughout the archipelago. And soon afterwards, the revolutionary leaders founded the Republic of the Philippines on June 12, 1898.

However, the U.S. refused to recognize the Republic, and in a Proclamation of Benevolent Assimilation, the U.S. President announced the government's intention to annex the Philippines. To make it legal, the U.S. paid Spain 20 million silver pesos–or two silver pesos per Filipino.

Impotent and defeated, Spain had no right to hand the islands over in the Treaty of Paris, since they were already independent at that point. So the Philippine-American war, billed here as a mere native insurgency, raged for the next decade. Literally half of the U.S. Army came to lay waste to any and all resistance. Whole towns were decimated by famine and disease, not to mention the slash-and-burn techniques that would return in the Vietnam War. The Filipino dead numbered at least 250,000, and "Luzon lost one-eighth of its population."[19] Clearly that "benevolent assimilation" was anything but.

In the century since, the price of a Filipina has not kept pace at all with the rate of inflation. Instead of being worth 2 silver pesos a head, the sex industry offers "a girl for the price of a burger"–or, more crudely put, "little brown fucking machines powered by rice." The numbers of registered sex workers and "entertainment" operations keeps growing, sucking in women and children, sometimes as young as 7 or 8 years old.

> According to IBON Databank, a private research institution, there are approximately 500,000 women prostitutes. Of these, the UNICEF says 20% or 100,000 are children, distributed in 37 provinces all over the country. The Philippines now ranks fourth among nine countries with the most number of prostituted children.
>
> It is, therefore, not very good for our national pride that even *Fortune Magazine* has designated the Philippines as a leading sex site on the Net.[20]

Virginity is a premium commodity in this economy of shame as insurance against infection–but only for the "customer." These workers literally bear the weight of colonial history and neo-imperialist policies on their knees and on their backs. Of course, with the sex trade come other social costs such as physical and emotional abuse from pimps and johns (including pedophiles), unwanted pregnancies, sexually transmitted diseases, and deepened poverty. And when public authorities respond to community complaints, it is usually with raids on the victims rather than the victimizers, the customers. And in the few instances when they do pursue the victimizers, they shut down the small fry and the bigger businesses, which are usually foreign-owned, go untouched. Desire in its crudest form is thus reified, commodified, and super/imposed on the bodies of women.

But the sex industry is not the only face of the Miss Saigon syndrome. There are other costs of militarization and globalization–costs that make a war on poverty a war instead on the poor or otherwise marginalized. For instance, there is the ongoing debate over contraception, abortion, and population control, with women's bodies as contested sites. There is the active repression over the desperate need for land reform and an economy that can harness all the energy and talent of its people. Families are evicted and communities dislocated in search of work while properties pass into or remain in the hands of multinational corporations and big landlords whose very presence is at-will and whose appetites run unchecked. There are the overly rosy estimations of economic development packages like Philippines 2000 (only the latest and largest of many as before now)–packages whose negative social, economic, and environmental impacts will be borne disproportionately by women.

So Miss Saigon is not just on stage, but also in the streets and statistics. Militarization and globalization engender misery.

SEE ALSO: *"entertainment,"women in; foreign investment; mail-order brides; militarization and demilitarization; myth of equal citizenship; orientalism; sex tours; white man's burden.*

FLOR CONTEMPLACIÓN

Flor Contemplación is the domestic worker sentenced to death and killed in Singapore in March 1995 for the alleged murder of another maid and her charge. For our purposes, I am not primarily concerned with the torture she suffered at the hands of the Singaporean government or how the Philippine government ultimately proved impotent to protect her, dramatic and regrettable as her story is. I am more concerned with what She represents and the fact that her story is yet relived millions of times over. The sexual oppression and violence wrought under colonial rule persists in this neocolonial era as economic violence of the highest order–legitimated by the glossy ideal of globalization. For a variety of reasons, the Philippines is a nation that cannot support all the people it educates, let alone the unskilled or the poorest of the poor.

The apparent solution to the "cash flow problem," from the smallest village to the halls of Malacañang Palace, is the availability of "cheap, repressed, and flexible labor"[21] for hire domestically or abroad as overseas contract workers (OCWs), often for jobs demanding little skill and offering poor work conditions. Let us examine how this translates into sheer numbers. Of this population of 70 million:

- 70% of the people suffer malnutrition
- the per capita annual income is $570
- unemployment is at 8.6%, but underemployment is at 26%
- the total foreign debt is $34.4 billion, with interest payments of $4 billion per year
- for every professional who stays, three join the army of export labor
- 7.2 million Filipinos work overseas in 130 countries; 55% of these are women
- 2000 leave the country *each day* as OCWs, and 200,000 women are exported each year
- OCWs remit $5 billion per year, up from $1 billion in 1990.[22]

Whether as raw numbers or even as estimates, these statistics are staggering and depressing, and after a while the cumulative pain becomes as unbearable as it is undeniable.

Those who go abroad are especially vulnerable to exploitation, both physical and economic. Many seek this work even illegally (further restricting their options and access to resources), using forged papers or tourist visas to leave the country first and then secure work permits later. Both the Philippines and the receiving nations offer them few legal protections; they are at the mercy of their "employers"–or husbands, in the case of mail-order brides–to honor their commitments with fairness, if at all. Benefits and social services are few, hard to find, or sometimes nonexistent. Workers are discouraged from forming unions to protect their own interests or often isolated from other networks that could help them reduce or avoid the exploitation that they risk. Labor advocates and relief agencies report that women OCWs usually experience the worst kind of abuse. Complaints range from non-payment of wages to long work hours (beyond the contract), from bad work conditions to maltreatment from employers. Cases of death abroad are not always suicides as reported; quite a few are suspected victims of torture and abuse. With 40,000 complaints lodged in 1995, one can only imagine what has gone unreported. Meanwhile, the country is so dependent on the remittances sent back home that it generally fails to protect its own people, doing instead whatever it can to maintain smooth relations with the countries who import the laborers.

The social cost of these sacrifices is just as staggering. Native societies are destabilized and disfigured in all the flux. Families are particularly hard hit. What Rhacel Parreñas calls "the international transference of mothering" is a sad irony: for months and sometimes years at a time, Filipinas leave their own children behind to care for the children of first-world–or at least richer–parents.[23] Sacrifices like this can never be entirely recouped.

In doing research for this paper, I came across a prayer for overseas contract workers that was especially touching, for it draws on a deep spring of faith to speak to the cares and needs of workers–especially female workers–as they leave to follow through on difficult choices made for the sake of their families. They pray for safe passage to their destination, that their jobs and employers will be decent, that they will be spared harm or humiliation, and that their sacrifices will not be in vain. Most of all they pray for safe passage back home.

SEE ALSO: *anti-Asian violence; Balabagan, Sarah; domestic violence; feminization of poverty; "free trade;" globalization; IMF/ World Bank; labor export policies; overseas contract workers (OCWs); structural adjustment policies (SAPs); underdevelopment.*

So as we confront both the glories and the shames of our past and present, what do we choose to remember? What do–or should–we try to forget?

Even this cursory, admittedly selective review of Philippine history prior to–and since–colonization shows that feminist issues and issues of nationhood and the common good are inextricably bound together. At the risk of overly romanticizing the precolonial past, we nonetheless see women and communities in right relation as shown through the examples of the *babaylanes,* tribal leaders, and insurrectionists like Gabriela Silang. However, when the nation does not order its priorities rightly–when women (and the land) are put second, when Western-style capitalist consumption is presented and accepted as the feasible only escape from colonial legacies–the nation suffers. Colonial mestiza flowers such as Maria Clara, unwitting victims of militarization such as Miss Saigon, and pawns such as Flor Contemplación in the game of neo-imperialist globalization are indeed icons of Filipina womanhood's underside. More than mere fictions or popular rallying cries, they reflect real struggles that real Filipinas have had to face not only in the past one hundred years, but in the past four hundred. They remind us of a history that cannot be ignored.

Politics and finance aside, the physical effects of colonialism are clearly visible–in the streets, in the families, in the ravaged land. Meanwhile, the psychic toll of colonialism is collective insecurity, even self-hatred. I am reminded of a woman I once interviewed for an earlier work. Born Filipina Catholic, she underwent religious conversions that paralleled her political ones. First she became what she called a fundamentalist Protestant, and some years later converted to orthodox Judaism. At a certain point in her faith journey she had asked herself: *what kind of God is this Christian God, this Catholic God who has done nothing to reverse or even ease the misery of the people.* And she found comfort and strength in what she called the justice narratives of the Torah. For her, her salvation lay, in part, in casting aside a religious system that she found a dead end, a way of living and believing that she found incoherent and senseless.

One can always point fingers in this pimping of a nation: driven by the need to alleviate its grinding poverty, the Philippines has made Faustian deals with the tourist industry, foreign military forces, and Western-imposed fiscal policies. In the process, land, labor, beauty, and flesh are all commodified. Blinded by the twin false promises of commercialism and consumption, the nation chokes. And while the Church offers solace to many, the people as a whole still suffer poverty on multiple levels: of mind, of spirit, of educational and employment opportunities, of dignity and justice.

All this has not been intended as a blanket or scattershot rant against what Spain and the U.S. hath wrought in their conflations of religion and politics. I do not want to demonize the colonial powers that were, are, and probably will be; nor do I want to stigmatize the Philippine people as being irreversibly paralyzed in this dysfunctional relationship. And regardless of religious or political stance or economic status, no one on any side is absolved of complicity–even if unwitting–in perpetuating these systems of injustice. Cultural differences discovered do not excuse oppression, and they certainly do not legitimate violence. But if we–as ethicists, people of faith, or simply people of good will–are to hold to the ideals of love, justice, and compassion, we must give them breath and shape through acts of solidarity both symbolic and substantive. It is not just a question of minimizing harm anymore; it is a question of atoning, of healing, of making things right. We should support movements of resistance, reconciliation, and transformation when the cause is just and legitimate. We need to keep in mind that multiple facets of sexual oppression–historical, political, social, economic, religions, and ethnic–will often demand simultaneous attention. And certainly we should do our part in healing both sides of victimhood, keeping the goal of redistributive justice in sight. Filipinas' issues pertain to all levels of community, including the national, the global, and the ecclesiastical.

As the churches fumble with positions on precisely those issues that affect women, they are challenged to redirect their energy away from so much moralizing, for moralizing alone does not effect healthy moral development. Instead, they need to engage in a constructive, concrete embodiment of the prophetic: really taking a hard look at moral dilemmas forced by tough choices, really sticking up for the poor, really being critical of injustice, really questioning the absurdities of double standards and doublespeak . . . and really acting up as warranted. For example, why *not* make the next liberation project the pursuit of liberation from development? For the good of the Filipina and the good of the people as a whole, to model and champion right relationship in this profoundly fractured context would be a most wonderful revolutionary act.

NOTES

1. Cited in Lawrence T. Johnson, "The Migration Waves of Filipinos," *Rice* 1:11 (July 1988), 37-39.

2. In Asian/Pacific-American communities especially since 1965, first-generation immigrants are the *adults* who come over; their U.S.-born offspring are the second generation. However, a 1.5-generation immigrant is one who was born in the country of origin and then immigrated to the receiving nation as a child or adolescent. It implies having "both/and" and "neither/nor" aspects in cultural identification and experience.

3. In this latter period I also include the brief yet brutal Japanese occupation during World War II.

4. José Rizál, *Noli me tangere*, trans. Ma. Soledad Lacson-Locsin, ed. Raul L. Lacson (Honolulu: University of Hawaii Press, 1997), xiii.

5. Delia D. Aguilar, "Lost in Translation: Western Feminism and Asian Women," in *Dragon Ladies*, ed. Sonia Shah (Boston: South End, 1997), 160-161.

6. In this section, I rely greatly on the collections of Mary John Mananzan and materials provided by the GABRIELA Network.

7. Mary John Mananzan, "The Filipino Woman: Before and After the Spanish Conquest of the Philippines," in *Essays on Women* (Women's Studies Series no. 1),

revised ed., ed. Mary John Mananzan (Manila: Institute of Women's Studies, St. Scholastica's College, 1991), 11.

8. In her introductory essay to *Woman and Religion*, revised ed., ed. Mary John Mananzan (Manila: Institute of Women's Studies, St. Scholastica's College, 1992), 3. Mananzan explains this through an etymology: " . . . the word for God, *Bathala*, does not have a sexist connotation. In the primitive Tagalog script, the word 'god' is made up of three consonants *Ba-Tha-La*. The first consonant is the first syllable of the word *babae* (woman) which symbolizes generation. The third consonant is the first syllable of *lalake* (man) which symbolizes potency. They are joined by the middle consonant, an aspirated H which means light or spirit. The word therefore, means the union of man and woman in light. And when one reads the word backwards, it reads *LahatBa*, meaning total generation, total creator ('to do,' *'creador'*). In other words, the concept of god among the ancient Tagalogs was more closely linked with woman; and, when linked with both the concepts of man and woman, there is nuance of union and mutuality, not subordination."

9. Carolyn Cervantes Aquino et al., "The Philippines: History, Imperialism, and Resistance," *kaWOMENan* (Summer 1998), 2.

10. Marina G. Espina's research on the Filipino Cajuns makes the connections. "Manilamen" pressed into harsh service on board jumped ship, settled and intermarried in places such as Acapulco and Veracruz, and even crossed the gulf to go as far east as Louisiana, just shy of the New Orleans area. Linguistically they could blend in quite easily. By her count, Filipinos have been on American soil for about ten generations now. Cf. the summary in Fred Cordova, *Filipinos: Forgotten Asian Americans* (Seattle: Demonstration Project for Asian Americans, 1983), 1-7.

As further proof of the transpacific link, there is Nuestra Señora de la Paz y Buenviaje (Our Lady of Peace and Good Voyage, the Virgin of Antipolo). Governor-General Juan Niño de Tabor of Acapulco brought it to the Philippines in 1626.

Oddly enough these ties that are being renewed and sustained as peoples of Spain's former colonies (Philippines and most of Latin America) encounter each other in communities here in the U.S.

11. Vicente L. Rafael, *Contracting Colonialism: Translation and Christian Conversion in Tagalog Society Under Early Spanish Rule* (Durham, NC: Duke UP, 1993), 18-19.

12. Until very late, Spaniards called the Malays *Indio* as a pejorative. *Filipino* first referred to a Spaniard or Spanish *mestizo* born in the Philippines, as opposed to a *Peninsular* who was born in Spain proper. *Filipino* did not begin taking on its contemporary meaning as a marker of national identity until Rizál's era.

13. Rafael, 84-109.

14. Mananzan, "Women and Religion," 7.

15. Mananzan, "Women and Religion," 7-8.

16. Mananzan, "Women and Religion," 8.

17. "One Hundred Years of Producing and Reproducing the Filipino," *Amerasia Journal* 24:2 (1998), 3.

18. For brief accounts on the VFA, see Walden Belo, "What's Between the Lines? A Commentary on US-RP Visiting Forces Agreement," *Filipina* (October 1998), 26-27, 89; Jowel F. Canuday, "Sex Workers Launch Drive Against VFA Ratifica-

tion," *Philippine Daily Inquirer* (18 September 98); Martin P. Marfil, "Senate Nod on VFA Uncertain," *Philippine Daily Inquirer* (12 October 98); Roland G. Simbulan, *A Status of Forces Agreement (SOFA) by Another Name: An Overview and Salient Points* (Manila: Nuclear Free Philippines Coalition, 1998). Not surprisingly, the VFA has registered little mention in mainstream US news.

19. Aquino, 3.

20. Olive Ranido, "Liberalizing the Flesh Trade," *GABRIELA Women's Update* 7:1 (Jan-Mar 1998), 14.

21. Center for Women Resources, "APEC: Implementing GATT-WTO in the Asia-Pacific. Increased Oppression and Exploitation for Women," (Quezon City, 24 November 96) 5-8; Liza Largoza-Maza, "The Impact of Imperialist Globalization: Displacement, Commodification, and Modern-Day Slavery of Women," 8-10.

22. Compiled from multiple GABRIELA Network reports and press releases.

23. Rhacel Salazar Parreñas, dissertation in progress, University of California, Berkeley.

Response to Essays
on "Remembering Conquest"

Mary E. Hunt

The pioneering work of these four scholars opens a new era in anti-violence efforts. No longer can any such work, especially in religious circles, afford to be done without explicit attention to an analysis of and commitment to eradicate colonializing elements. This focus on the many faces of colonialism makes clear that particularity cannot be lost in this quest for justice. I appreciate the essays as a running start in the right direction. I am honored to add my response to the mix. I will make a brief comment on each one, and then focus on action steps each essayist implies for people in religiously based social change groups. While I would have liked all of the essays to have more explicit analyses of the religious issues at hand, I am grateful that they provide a strong foundation on which future scholars and activists can build.

Traci West's fine paper comes on the heels of the recent revelations about President Thomas Jefferson having fathered a child with a slave woman. While the discourse in this regard has linked him with President Bill Clinton, the smart money is on the fact that he was a rapist. As NPR commentator B.B. Campbell pointed out, in Jefferson's day a slave woman could not say no to a white man, no young girl of 14 was free to deny sexual pleasure to an adult man, and surely few women were free to turn down the President. Perhaps the parallels with Mr. Clinton are deeper than we have probed but that is a subject for another piece.

[Haworth co-indexing entry note]: "Response to Essays on 'Remembering Conquest.' " Hunt, Mary E. Co-published simultaneously in *Journal of Religion & Abuse* (The Haworth Pastoral Press, an imprint of The Haworth Press, Inc.) Vol. 1, No. 2, 1999, pp. 71-77; and: *Remembering Conquest: Feminist/Womanist Perspectives on Religion, Colonization, and Sexual Violence* (ed: Nantawan Boonprasat Lewis and Marie M. Fortune) The Haworth Pastoral Press, an imprint of The Haworth Press, Inc., 1999, pp. 71-77. Single or multiple copies of this article are available for a fee from The Haworth Document Delivery Service [1-800-342-9678, 9:00 a.m. - 5:00 p.m. (EST). E-mail address: getinfo@haworthpressinc.com].

West makes clear that colonialism is not an umbrella category useful in all cases, indeed that it does not fit neatly for African Americans whose history differs from that of colonized people. This is a note of caution for those who would incorporate colonialism into their interstructured analysis without nuance, simply adding it to a laundry list without specificity. One clear message from all of these papers is that just adding colonialism to a list of racism, classism and sexism and thinking one has done the job is inadequate. Particular problems require particular solutions.

Her most challenging point, in my judgement, is her insistence that efforts by those in the helping professions, and here I would include pastoral counselors as well as psychologists, must take account of the white supremacist foundations on which even the best sexual assault programs are built. I envision well-intentioned religious professionals helping/healing/fixing, even trying to prevent sexual violence, without for a moment understanding the complexity of West's compelling argument. I take her insight as the first step toward an important new anti-racist hermeneutic, a new lens of analysis that every such program needs to employ before repeating the mistakes of old. This will not be easy, and it will require the analytic sophistication of this essay and more to bring it about.

I suggest that those who seek to eradicate violence from religious starting points put anti-racism at the top of the agenda in theoretical and practical discussions especially in Christian organizations. The extra layers of Christian colonialism and Christian racism need to be problematized. Religious colonialism as such is not part of Traci West's analysis in this work. But some of the dynamics she outlines with regard to African American women's well-being in a racist society parallel most women's treatment in Christian churches. Without in any way backing off of a critique of racism, I propose the application of this analysis by extension to dismantle gender-based oppression built into the so-called helping relationships.

West's constructive work needs to be applied to Jewish, Muslim and other religiously based efforts to eradicate violence. It will be resisted, as those who, including well-intentioned liberals, do not want to change fundamental assumptions, resist many anti-racist efforts. But no program can afford to leave it aside if it is serious about eliminating violence. The second wave of anti-violence work begins here.

Read in tandem with Traci West's work, Andrea Smith's powerful essay makes many of the same points with regard to the need to be very specific about the impact of colonialism. She, like West, underscores the stunning power of colonialism to destroy self-esteem, therefore destroy a people from the inside out. Her claim that "struggles for sovereignty" for Native peoples are undermined by "the inability to address sexual violence" is a clarion call for attention to these matters as well as a methodological innovation in this justice work.

Through horrendous data, Andrea Smith makes clear the multivalent dimensions of colonialism with regard to Native peoples. The catalogue of physical and psychological harms includes the specific oppression of Native women who live with disabilities, an important reminder that indeed all women with disabilities are subject to hideous violence, but that Native women live with an added burden in this regard.

The impact on children of the robbery of self-esteem by colonizers is reminiscent of Traci West's point about what happens to African Americans. And the data on astronomical cancer rates among children growing up in the Four Corners region is enough to persuade the most recalcitrant that genocide continues with abandon.

I was especially struck by Andrea Smith's argument that Native women are both a symbol of degradation and themselves degraded as described in her comments about the stereotypes of dirt. This self-fulfilling nature of colonialist discourse undoubtedly has other manifestations as well. I wonder if Native men are subject to rape and other forms of sexual abuse, and if so how one interprets such information in this schema. In addition, I wondered how the attitude "The feds will take care of it" with regard to "community response to sexual violence" might contribute to the problem. It seems even more deeply vexing for the reasons Traci West pointed out, namely, that such efforts, in this case piecemeal and untrustworthy, are themselves fraught with the colonizing assumptions that prevent real change.

What can religious communities do to address these grievous problems? First, there is a need to take a critical look at the images, or lack thereof, of the Native peoples that are held commonly within different religious traditions. If Andrea Smith is correct, and I see no evidence to the contrary, the very images and symbols of Native peoples, especially Native women, that undergird the colonizing structures require overhaul. What better place to begin than with how religions have framed them, since we have the hermeneutical tools to disassemble and reconstruct them according to the dictates of the persons themselves.

Second, how do we bring religious sensibilities to community-based justice work in the face of the growing prison-industrial complex? It may be that the foundational work to stem the tide will be religious in character, as it is religions, not laws or businesses, which specialize in justice, mercy and forgiveness. A related problem is how to bring the discussion of sexual violence into conversations about sovereignty, a challenge that religious people will need to join if change is expected.

Nantawan Lewis deals with similar issues, albeit in an entirely different context. Her insightful review of the Thai situation is shockingly similar to that of U.S. African American and Native experiences, complete with U.S. military to undergird the oppression. I was relieved to read that she values tears in response to the horrors of the situation. Sometimes scholars react by increasing the distance between themselves and their subjects, or by engaging in abstraction to remain inured to the horrors. But tears indicate that this researcher is engaged and able to name what she sees for what it is.

The central role of HIV/AIDS in the Thai situation both marks it as unique and connects it with so many other cultures, especially in Africa where the pandemic is raging. Heterosexual male to female transmission makes HIV/AIDS another example of sexual oppression turned deadly. The UNAIDS/WHO reports that HIV/AIDS spread among upper class as well as poor people in developing countries is increasing. Newly affluent men who can finally afford to have what other men have, namely, women prostitutes, are at high risk. Development is expensive and sometimes deadly.

The Centers for Disease Control in the U.S. report that countries like India and China with their huge populations have only seen the tip of the iceberg in terms of numbers of people infected with HIV/AIDS. Worse yet, social services, especially for immigrants, are so lacking in the U.S. that some people find themselves "better off" infected than not. Tears do not suffice to respond to such a tragedy, but they are a start.

Dr. Lewis makes clear that prostitution is an ancient practice but a new form of colonialization as practiced in Thailand. The feminist theological response by Thai scholar Dr. Suwanna Satha-Anand is a helpful antidote. Such reworkings of Buddhist thought, like their

Christian, Jewish, Muslim and other counterparts, are essential to justice work of this sort. In other work, Dr. Satha-Anand reported that 60% of the Thai budget is made up of sex tourism. What will replace it as an economic entity? This is as important a question in the practical order as what causes it. Thus, the connection between anti-violence work and economic policies begs feminist theological attention. Scholarly attention to both issues–economics and violence–is called for.

My suggestions for action are again quite concrete. I invite further reflection on what this experience in Thailand means for Thai people living in the U.S., for example. I see some transfer value to the ideas and strategies. Moreover, I wonder how colonialization in the U.S. changes the focus and complicates the situation for Thai women living in a culture that is so different from their own. Answers to these questions are necessary for adequate pastoral practice.

The complexity of interreligious factors here leads me to recommend that all religious anti-violence work in the future be done in a multi-religious fashion. The U.S. population is increasingly more diverse religiously, requiring increasing sophistication on the part of anti-violence advocates who previously worked in one tradition only. For example, feminist liberation work in Buddhism is a welcome addition to a conversation that for too long has been almost exclusively Christian and Jewish. It is useful not only for working with Buddhists, but also for thinking religiously from other starting points about violence.

Imagine if HIV/AIDS and domestic violence were to become the most pressing ecumenical topics of the moment. They would eclipse matters of intercommunion and shared sanctuaries in airports that have made so much interreligious dialogue so fruitless in the last decade. The very urgency of these problems might hasten the overdue results of interfaith work that now languish for lack of interest. As feminist anti-violence advocates take up the job I am confident that it must be interreligious or risk being irrelevant.

Rachel Bundang's useful paper adds another dimension to the challenge. Like Traci West and Andrea Smith, she outlines a specific situation with specific consequences. The Filipino experience is not the African American or Native American one, but one that is also deeply influenced by its historical particularity. Like Nantawan Lewis, she shows how the U.S. military continues to undergird the oppression. She demonstrates how U.S. corporations bolster an economy built on the backs of women. This analysis can be extended to the many places where the military reaches, adding another layer of concern for those who do anti-violence work. Women abused by military men need to be understood and helped in light of militarism. Only then will the full scope of the cause and possible cure be understood.

The global aspects at hand are chilling. The fact that "Miss Saigon" is played so successfully by a Filipina is an example of the "interchangeable" way in which people from Asia are treated, as if the particularity of their own country were unimportant. Such a move in a culture of objectification is colonializing in the extreme.

The religious aspect of this analysis intrigued me. I wonder where the values of "love, justice and solidarity" come from that does not lead to hegemonic Christian claims. I promote such values, naming them as part of my Christian history and tradition. But this essay reminds me of the serious need to check assumptions at the door when engaging in the multi-religious movement against violence that I think these essays suggest is necessary for the future.

On the basis of Rachel Bundang's helpful analysis, I suggest that anti-violence advocates look critically at the Filipino population in the U.S. to see how aspects of this history and culture are neglected in efforts to be helpful in their struggles. The same would be true among Chinese, Japanese, Korean and other immigrants whose particular cultures are finally quite different despite the blurring of the lines by those who see all Asians as alike. The danger of this approach, not to mention its rank racism, is now obvious. The second wave of religiously founded anti-violence work will need to be more analytically and practically sophisticated, building on the fine work of the first wave, but realizing, as these essays demonstrate, that there is more at stake than anyone imagined.

Within a Christian framework, I encourage programmatic critiques of the tradition, especially in Catholic communities (for example, many Filipino groups are Catholic). Such inventories of the sexism of Christianity do not mean that one leaves it aside, rather that one makes use of the astute critiques of feminist, womanist and other women-affirming theologians so as to avoid the pitfalls of patriarchy. Such feminist theological insights are helpful in the struggle for "liberation from development" that underlies this analysis since they now include not simply a gender analysis, but one that takes account of white suprema-

cy, economic justice, heterosexism and discrimination based on physical ability. I insist on this approach because I am increasingly skeptical
about the ability and/or political will of patriarchal churches to do this
kind of work on their own. Because the results impinge so directly on
anti-violence work, I see no reason to take chances.

I appreciate the work of these scholars. I hope that my comments
and suggestions will add a useful, task-oriented–how to put this analysis into concrete practice in the religious world–focus. That way, these
various intellectual contributions toward religiously based social
change will be well used in the eradication of violence.

Index

Abuse of children. *See* Boarding schools; Rape
Abusive relationship, self-blame in, 23-24
Advertisements
characterizations of Native peoples in, 33
Ivory Soap, 33
Virginia Slims, 38-39
Africa, AIDS in, 74
African American history, colonialism and, 72
African American women, in racist society. *See* Sexual assault programs
Afro-American women. *See also* African American entries
history of rape, 22
Afro-Americans, U.S. indigenous identity of, 21
complexity similar to that of abused women, 21
Aggression, global capitalistic, impact on lives, 7-8
AIDS
Africa, 74
Chiang Mai (Thailand), prevalence, 7
Church of Christ, Office of AIDS Ministry, 7
religion as solution, 14
Thailand, 2,74
death rate in, 9
extramarital affairs and, 8
prostitution and, 8-9
Aldea Rio Negro (Guatemala), massacre of Mayan people in, in 1982, 36
American Academy of Religion Annual Meeting, Orlando, Florida, 1998, 1

American Indian women. *See also* Native peoples
genocide and, 3
mutilation of, 3
rape of, 3
sexual violence and, 3
violence against, 3
Anti-racism, Christian organizations and. *See* Sexual assault programs
Anti-racist movement, to end sexual violence, 29
Anti-rape movement, white-dominated, 32
Anti-violence advocates, Filipino population in U.S. and, 76
Anti-violence efforts
actions to take, 75
Christian churches and (*See* Sexual assault programs)
Christian outreach projects and, 28
colonizing elements addressed in, 71
concrete practice of, 77
religious work, multi-religious fashion for, 75
Asia. *See also* specific countries
people treated as interchangeable, 76
sex tourism in, 6-7

Babaylan
Filipina womanhood and, 53
Tagalog priestess, 56
Bathala, God as union of male and female spirit, 56
bell hooks, theories of, 25
BIA. *See* Bureau of Indian Affairs
Biblical Canaanites, likened to Native peoples, 34

Massacres
of indigenous peoples, U.S.
government funding of,
36-37
of Native peoples, 35
in Latin America, 36-37
in North America, 36
Mayan people, massacre (in 1982), 36
Mending the Hoop Technical
Assistance Project, MN,
Native community programs
and, 32
Militarism, as contributor to violence
against women, 2
Militarization
costs of, 63
U.S. presence in Philippines and,
61
Military installations, sex industry
and, 60-61
Ministry of Foreign Affairs, Thai
victim presenting case to, 7
Miss Saigon
character played by Filipina, 76
Filipina experience, 3
Filipina womanhood and, 53
icon of Filipina womanhood, 65-66
as victim of militarization, 65-66
Miss Saigon (musical)
problematic nature of, 60
story line, 60
Miss Saigon syndrome, sex industry
and, 63
Mohawk crisis, Oka, description of, 37
Muslims, Spanish incursions and, in
Mindanao, 56-57
Mutilation
of Indian bodies, 35
accounts of, 36
of indigenous women's bodies, in
Latin America, 36-37

National Council of Churches, Office
of Justice for Women and, 1
Native bodies

equated with dirt, Ivory Soap ad,
33
seen as polluted with sexual sin, 34
Native communities, sexual violence
within, 31
boarding school and, 43
Native domestic violence
pressures on survivors, 44-45
tribal mediation programs and,
44-45
Native Hawaiian culture, cultural
prostitution of, 42
Native peoples. *See also* American
Indian women
"absence" of, 33
characterization of by white
Californians, 33
colonizers' views
sexual perversity of, 34
sexual sin and, 34
colonizing structures, 73-74
religions and, 73-74
domestic violence advocates and,
44
genocide, sexual violence as tool
of, 31, 32
mass sterilization of Native women,
in 1970s, 34-35
massacres of, 35
oppression faced within criminal
justice system, 44
portrayal by dominant culture,
40-41
sexual violence against, 31-32,37
struggles for sovereignty, 73
Native spiritual traditions
appropriation of, 42
sexual overtones and, 42
Native women
abuse of, 39-40
boarding school experience of,
39-40
colonization of, 39-40
instances of, 37
experience of sexual abuse
survivors, 39-40

militaristic
colonization of Thailand and, 9
role in sex industry, 8
U.S. government, agreement with
Philippines, 61
U.S. military
abuse of women and, 75-76
bases in Thailand, growth of sex
tourism and, 8-9
oppression and, 74-76
U.S. slavery, differentiated from third
world colonization, 21

Vessantara jataka tale, cultural
empowerment of women
and, 15-16
Victim-survivor,
colonizing/missionary
message for, 28
Video game, subjugation of Indian
women's bodies in, 37-38
Vietnam War, and Thailand, U.S.
military bases in, 8-9
Violence Against Women, conference,
Toronto, Canada, 1996, 1
Violence against women. *See* Sexual
violence
not regarded as crime, 46
traditional alternatives to
incarceration for, 44-45
U.S. presence in Philippines and,
61
Virginity, as commodity, 62
Vocational skills, need to provide
alternative, 15-16

Wall, Jeffrey, sexual abuse as part of
Native ritual and, 42-43
War crimes tribunal, against Serbs, 37
White Christian colonizers, American
Indian experience with, 3
White dominance, racial myths and,
26
White domination, self-blame and, 25
White racist mobs, harassment of
Native women and, 37
White standard, measuring blacks, 25
White supremacy
Christian framework for, 76-77
context for Black women and, 3
psycho-social captivity of Black
women, 2
rape and, 23
Wilson, Melba, incest survivor, 24
Women
Native, as bearers of
counter-imperial order, 35
white, as bearers of more racist
imperial order, 35
Women Against Rape (London),
statement regarding criminal
justice system, 48
Women Foundation of Thailand, 6
Women's Desk, World Council of
Churches, 1
Women's inferiority
role of Buddhism in accepting, 13
Thai feudalism and, 12-13
World Bank, currency crisis in
Thailand and, 10